COLIN DYE is Senior Pastor at Kensington Temple, London. Born in Kenya, East Africa, in 1953, he came to London to train for a career in the performing arts. Two years later he became a Christian and in 1975 he left his successful career to attend Bible college. By this time a member at Kensington Temple, he entered the ministry as Assistant Pastor in 1979, the year in which he married Amanda. Six years later, after pastoring a church in Bournemouth and obtaining the Bachelor of Divinity degree, he was called back to Kensington Temple as Associate Pastor. In 1991, he was appointed Senior Pastor. A gifted communicator, Colin Dye frequently ministers at international conferences. His passion for evangelism and mission takes him all over the world, but alongside London and Britain, he has a special burden for Africa and South America.

Prayer Explosion

Power for
Christian living

Colin Dye

Hodder & Stoughton
LONDON SYDNEY AUCKLAND

British Library Cataloguing in Publication Data
A record for this book is available from the British Library

ISBN 0 340 64206 8

Printed and bound in Great Britain by
Cox & Wyman Ltd, Reading, Berkshire

Hodder and Stoughton
A division of Hodder Headline PLC
338 Euston Road
London NW1 3BH

To all those who are part of this story: the often unseen intercessors of Kensington Temple who have been faithful over several generations, the past and present leaders of our church and my praying friends, many of them now scattered across the globe watching and waiting for the coming revival.

Contents

Acknowledgements

In preparing this material for publication I recognise how much I owe those who have not only worked closely with me on the project but also those who have either directly or indirectly influenced my prayer life. Many of these people have been mentioned in the book, but perhaps no one has been a greater source of inspiration and encouragement than Suzette Hattingh from Reinhard Bonnke's ministry, Christ for all Nations. Suzette led a life-changing week of prayer in Kensington Temple in 1987. It set the seal on what God had been doing among us for many years and it also fleshed things out for the future. I know how profoundly so many people were affected by her visit and the fresh impetus the church received at that time. My more solid thinking about prayer and intercession really began at that time.

Now coming to the book itself, I really must pay full tribute to Barbara Hills. I am most fortunate to have had such a talented writer to help me put my thoughts on to paper. I am primarily a teacher and preacher and changing the spoken word into the written word is not easy. Barbara has done an admirable job. Not only has she helped me convey exactly what I wanted to say, she has been an 'active ingredient' in the whole process.

I am also grateful to my family and friends for their patience and encouragement as I have gone off into long periods of silence (often alone) or picked their brains incessantly during the course of this project. Desmond Cartwright, who is probably Britain's most

informed scholar in Pentecostal history, has kept a
helpful eye on the matters of history I have briefly
touched upon. The story of the early Pentecostal leaders, their work in Britain and Europe and our debt as
evangelical and charismatic Christians is yet to be fully
told. Finally, I want to thank my prayer partners who
uphold me constantly. What you read in this book is as
much the result of their work as it is mine.

Introduction

When someone heard that I was thinking of writing this book they protested forcefully, 'Oh no! Not yet another book on prayer!' It is a fair comment as there has never been so much available on this subject as there is right now. This is of course God's doing, as he is stirring up his people to pray and prepare for revival. Any contribution to the current world prayer movement is set to line up with the present-day purposes of the Holy Spirit.

Despite these extensive publications on prayer I still find people struggling even with some of the basics! Why should we pray? What is prayer? How can we overcome the obstacles? What about warfare prayer? How about intercession? Prayer is without a doubt our single greatest spiritual weapon so why don't we do it more often and when we do how can we be effective in it? While these questions remain in our minds we will probably never come into the full delight that God calls us to enjoy with him in prayer.

Prayer is a relationship, a matter of abiding in Christ: 'If you remain in me and my words remain in you, ask whatever you wish, and it will be given you' (John 15:7). This emphasises the relational nature of prayer and sharply contrasts with the mechanical approach frequently given to it today.

So often, prayer is brought up in a desperate attempt to force us out of our guilt-ridden prayerlessness, but this only serves to deepen the problem. I have tried to avoid that by giving more on the practical 'how to' than on the motivational 'got to'. You and I don't need any books to tell us we ought to pray more; as it is we know that all too well!

This book is a story of how prayer works – not just in principle, but in reality. It is not about prayer alone but about the twin-turbo approach of prayer and evangelism. Nothing else can be substituted for this divinely ordained partnership of power. It is a marriage made in heaven and we must never separate one from the other.

Over the years in Kensington Temple we have witnessed some of the most remarkable church growth and spiritual happenings in Britain. If we had to isolate any one factor contributing to this outcome, it would be without a doubt, prayer. The secrets we have begun to discover are not new; they have been around for a very long time. It is simply opportune to bring them once more to the forefront of our thinking and our doing.

I have followed these principles closely as they have unfolded for around twenty-five years, trying to submit myself to the Holy Spirit's tutoring. It hasn't been easy and I tremble at the thought that some may be led in reading this book to consider my prayer life a model for other Christians. Only God and I know how truly inadequate that would be.

In releasing this material to the wider body of Christ, my prayer is that we should come to know him better in the secret place of intimacy with him. And that this will mean we move forward in prayer by leaps and bounds. The result of sharpening the cutting edge of our evangelism by effective prayer could well be that many thousands of people are released to find Christ. Having seen the results in our own church and having taught these principles all over the world, I am bold enough to believe that it can happen to you as well.

Colin Dye
London

1 Prayer Works

Revival secrets

In the space of a little over twenty years Kensington Temple (KT to its members) has grown from a church of three hundred members to around ten thousand people, meeting in up to six different Sunday services and over one hundred satellite churches all across London. During this time I have been a church member, a deacon, an elder, and am now the senior minister. Having witnessed this life and growth at first hand, I want to pass on to you here, in this book, its secrets – the spiritual keys that open spiritual doors.

Kensington Temple is one of the most cosmopolitan places in Britain, just one mile from London's Hyde Park. Situated in Notting Hill Gate, we receive people from all over the world. Over a hundred nationalities from every continent crowd into our services every Sunday. But we are just people, more or less like any others, with a complete mixture of traditions, a variety of jobs, interests, sorrows, struggles and joys. Yes, we have all discovered the reality of Jesus' resurrection and experienced the fullness of his life-giving Spirit, but so have a vast number of people in other churches. So what accounts for this remarkable expansion that shows no sign of slowing? It is undoubtedly

God's work. But why has God chosen to bless us so much?

There are many aspects to our rapid growth but the fundamental reason for it cannot be found in smooth organisation or advertising and marketing techniques or social action groups, as desirable as all of these may be. There is one Master Key. And the Master Key belongs to the Master himself who shares it with us. Behind every successful development, every creative plan and every thrust forward there is and has always been one thing – earnest, sustained prayer.

Prayer is the Master Key. It is of vital importance. I prize it above everything I do. If the Lord were to remove every other aspect of my ministry in public, leaving only my call to intercede, I would be fully satisfied. Prayer is the creative powerhouse of God within us. Prayer effects real change. Prayer transforms lives, churches and communities.

Kensington Temple began as a tiny band of people, less than fifty strong. But they were fifty people who took hold of God and God took hold of them. I would like to tell a little of how this happened. It's a story that could happen anywhere. All it takes are men and women open to share and respond to the desires of God's heart.

The story begins in the decade after the First World War. The initial jubilation of peace had passed and the coming depression of the thirties was having a grim impact on the life of everyone in Britain. Churches were struggling too. They were virtually empty. Nevertheless, Britain was about to experience a remarkable phenomenon.

Under the anointing of God's Spirit, two Welsh evangelists, George and Stephen Jeffreys, began to blaze a new trail for God across the nation. These men were known as Pentecostals, a new group of Christians who were rediscovering the power of the Holy Spirit. They proved to be tremendously effective evangelists, not because they were special in themselves but because they had learned a revival secret, the secret of powerful praying.

'Church full'

The events that followed the Jeffreys brothers around the country could have come straight from the book of Acts. Apostolic power was being released in a new wave of miraculous healings and in thousands of conversions. Called and set apart by the Lord, these evangelists dedicated their lives totally to the work of spreading the good news. This was the vision God had given them – to set people's hearts on fire for Christ and turn the nation back to God. They abandoned the trappings of the world and lived their vision.

At that time the power of the media as we know it didn't exist. The brothers couldn't rely on advertising alone. In fact, they often depended entirely on God to make his work known. They would arrive practically unannounced in a city, hire the largest hall and start their meetings.

In Birmingham, for example, the congregation on the opening day in 1930 had been minute. After several people were healed in the first few meetings numbers increased and within a short time the church building was packed to capacity. They had to move to another part of the city and hire a large skating rink. Even this was too small to cope with the crowds. The largest exhibition hall in the city was taken over and this too was packed to suffocation at times. Ten thousand made profession of salvation and hundreds claimed that they had been healed.

This was the power, released through prayer and evangelism, that began the church of Kensington Temple. The original name of this Victorian congregational church was Horbury Chapel. George's brother Stephen held meetings there. So many were healed that the papers called the church, the 'Bethesda of the West End'.

Ten years later, George bought the building and it continued as a place of prayer and healing. But then war-time conditions, the London blackout and the evacuation or call-up of many of the congregation seriously eroded their numbers. Disagreements over organisation and structures further sapped their energy. Finally the last surviving trustee was unable to continue and a small Pentecostal group under the leadership of Eldin Corsie was invited to take the building over.

Corsie was youthful, hopeful and yearning to see a new visitation of the Spirit of God in Notting Hill. As God would have it, the trustees wanted to sell Kensington Temple and approached the new church group who promptly bought it.

It must have been a daunting experience for that small congregation of around sixty as they entered Kensington Temple for their first service. One can imagine their thoughts as they looked around, dwarfed by a building designed to seat a thousand. They were well aware of the one-time success of the previous church and the realisation of the enormity of the challenge before them began to dawn.

'You have done it before, you can do it again. Lord, fulfil your word. Send people here from all over the world. May this church be like a city set on a hill.' This was Eldin Corsie's prayer of faith in 1965.

Then, during a session of spring-cleaning, Eldin and his helpers unearthed a sign that had been set outside the church during the revival. It read 'CHURCH

FULL'. In the basement they were astonished to discover, among the rubbish, a number of wheelchairs, crutches and other aids discarded by the sick when they had been healed. The sight of these reminders of the earlier revival under the Jeffreys brothers stunned everyone into the realisation of their need for God. They cried out in desperation, hungry for a new movement of the Spirit's power. An urgency entered their prayer meetings.

Hard ground

Outside the building things seemed to be getting worse not better. Notting Hill saw race riots, drug trafficking and prostitution. It was the swinging sixties, the era of drugs, sex and rock 'n' roll. Inside the church the believers were hard at prayer. They felt the spiritual confusion and emptiness all around them and sought God, pleading with him to act. And he did. One by one, lost, hungry and broken, people began to come in. Heroin-addicted, sexually disillusioned, lonely and frightened people alongside the wealthy and the secure-in-the-world, began to swell the congregation.

At the same time occult practitioners were very active in the area. A number of witches' covens were a stone's throw away from the church. One such follower, Audrey Harper, who came 'only for a cup of coffee', received such a warm welcome that she stayed and later went on to accept Jesus for herself. Other converts followed from all walks of life. Personalities from the media, political and sporting worlds all found their spiritual home. We were now in the seventies.

People from other nations, often rejected elsewhere, found acceptance in the congregation that now numbered over five hundred. Prayer had begun to break up the hard, unploughed ground of people's hearts. God was sending his showers. The harvest was ripening rapidly. The church at Notting Hill Gate was like an oasis in the middle of a wilderness. Week by week a core of eighty faithful people kept up the momentum of prayer and earnestly called on the Lord. The Spirit of God was powerfully present as, one by one, people stood in public prayer. Eldin encouraged us in those days with the words 'Prayer is the powerhouse of the Church'.

That was the KT I was introduced to. I took to it like a duck to water. It seemed as if it was what I'd been searching for all my life. It was 1972. I was a young student dancer in London and a new, enthusiastic convert to Christ. I had given my life to the Lord while on holiday, through the ministry of a tiny mission hall in the north of England. Once back in London I started to look for a church that could cope with my excitement, a place where I could grow spiritually and find out more about Jesus. Until this time I had found most churches boring and dull. As far as I was concerned they were irrelevant, never able to touch me where it mattered most in my life. I approached KT warily and, happily, had my illusions well and truly shattered.

The freedom of expression in the Holy Spirit was enthralling. The services were full of spontaneous praise and worship and I was filled with joy and an inexplicable delight just being among the congregation.

Real heroes

There were a few people that stood out to me even then as especially radiant members of the church. Their love for God seemed to shine out from their faces and in their every action. Everything about them spoke of their constant contact with the Lord. As I got to know them, I realised that the secret of this 'oneness' with Jesus was prayer. These people were the 'prayer warriors'.

It wasn't that they held public offices or were known and recognised for great achievements. In fact, most of them lived ordinary, mundane lives. Some worked in factories, others were office workers or cleaners and a number were elderly and retired. Their spiritual stature was largely unrecognised. Most of their prayers were prayed at home in secret. I soon discovered that their relationship with God was of paramount importance to these people. I would visit certain members of the church, sit down to a meal and find that a prayer of thanksgiving for the food would turn into a time of celebration and praise. Meals were always being reheated!

Spending time with someone you cannot see and addressing someone you cannot hear is not a high priority for the materially occupied. In fact it's incomprehensible, just so much foolishness, to the worldly-minded. Worldliness does not give up its stronghold easily and this attitude is often alive and well in the modern Christian mindset. It creeps into and overtakes our churches. Frantic activities, often legitimate in themselves, crowd out quality time with the Lord. External distractions are endless. Jobs, families, friendships, recreational pursuits as well as the endless round of Christian meetings, conferences and church commitments can all cram our lives leaving us exhausted and not feeling at all like praying. Any faint desire to seek God is soon dulled by long hours in front of the TV.

Then there are the inner barriers, the personal concerns, emotions and anxieties that accumulate like poison and attack our spiritual nervous systems. In such a paralysed, prayerless state, we deny ourselves God's antidote to the pressures of life: 'Do not be anxious about anything, but in everything, by prayer and petition, with thanksgiving, present your requests to God. And the peace of God, which transcends all understanding, will guard your hearts and minds in Christ Jesus' (Philippians 4:6–7).

Aware of the difficulties standing between ourselves and prayer, I am always deeply impressed by truly prayerful people. To me they are the unsung heroes, the real champions of the faith. The Pentecostal movement has had an ample share of them. They are not often publicly acclaimed or even particularly noticeable. They are usually the widows and the elderly spinsters, the shut-ins and the excluded. They rarely make it into the headlines but are well known in the heavenlies. Shunning all earthly fame they nevertheless feature prominently in God's 'Who's Who'. He is no respecter of persons. Once the Spirit of prayer comes into lives, even the most insignificant become real movers and shakers in the kingdom of God.

One such prayer warrior was Grace. Though well advanced in years, she gave herself tirelessly in service to the church. When arthritis prevented her from playing the piano in services, she devoted herself entirely to prayer and intercession. It cost her much effort and pain to stand before the Lord during the prayer meetings. But whenever she did, she was so full of the Lord that spiritual truths poured from her and she was barely able to keep up with herself.

'Bless-s-ed be the Lor-ord and S-saviour, Jes-s-us C-Christ!' she would stammeringly begin and, as she continued, the power of the Holy Spirit upon her would be so great that she'd look as if she was about to fall over. To people watching it was a comical sight but we soon came to appreciate the spiritual reality. Heaven seemed to come down in response to her prayer!

Grace's inspiration and example to us young people helped contribute to the environment in which our prayer lives could flourish. She, and people like her, also helped create the right spiritual climate for new initiatives of growth and evangelism.

Without prayer, evangelism is fruitless

Young people with an eagerness to evangelise began to flock to the church. Their energy was contagious. It wasn't long before we started a new all-night prayer meeting and evangelistic coffee bar. While one section of the church was at prayer another was out sharing faith on the streets of Notting Hill Gate. A remaining group was welcoming those who had been invited into the coffee bar. Prayer and evangelism went hand in hand, an effective, dynamic combination.

The modern church stresses techniques and methods in evangelism. In New Testament times the early Christians had none of these and yet they succeeded where we so often fail. We need to get back to the spiritual dynamics of New Testament evangelism.

The early believers in Jerusalem soaked everything they did in powerful prayer, especially evangelism. Opposed by the Sanhedrin, the highest Jewish court in the land, they stood up defiant in prayer. God was with them as they called out, 'Now, Lord, consider their threats and enable your servants to speak your word with great boldness' (Acts 4:29). Armed with a new boldness and a fresh infilling of the Holy Spirit, they went on to evangelise Jerusalem thoroughly. Every section of the city's population felt the effect, from the poor of the streets to the aristocratic priests of the Temple. This is the result of powerful prayer.

In those early days at Kensington Temple I was

learning priceless lessons. I could see that the conversions in the coffee bar and on the streets were a direct answer to those praying back in the church. While the workers were on the streets talking about their faith, the intercessors were crying out to God for the salvation of the very ones hearing the message of the gospel. Our praying was constantly updated by special 'runners' who went back and forth from the streets to the building. We often knew exactly who we were praying for and there were many outstanding conversions.

At the end of these long, tiring sessions we would all gather for a final cup of coffee and catch up on the full details of the night's 'fishing'. Then we would go home exhausted but brimming with excitement having seen God's power at work.

On one occasion we couldn't deal with a particularly tough nut. Someone brought a self-confessed atheist in from the streets. Very soon he had the whole team tangled up in his arguments. He was tying them in knots. In desperation the team leader dismissed him with a parting prayer, 'Lord, reveal yourself to this man.' A week later the man returned to tell his story.

After he had left the coffee bar, he had taken the team leader's prayer as a personal challenge to God. He had repeated it for himself and said, 'God, if you are real then show yourself to me.' Then he had laughed at himself for talking to God because, of course, God didn't exist, did he? No angel appeared to him, no sound of trumpet blasts filled the air and there were no fantastic miracles. In fact, by the time he reached his home he had forgotten all about the prayer.

The man took out his key and put it in the lock. He began to shake violently. For no apparent reason he suddenly grew aware of the supernatural presence of God. Hurrying into the house he immediately knelt down by his bed and turned his life over completely to the Lord Jesus. He got up a changed man!

Early lessons like these taught me that prayer really works! It was a discovery that went on to become the foundation of my life and ministry.

Ignorance of the battle is no protection against it

The more the church began to grow, the more attention we began to attract to ourselves – and not all of it was welcome. We became increasingly aware that there were disruptive influences in our meetings.

One Sunday morning during our worship service, a woman stood up and began to call out, 'Spirit of the world, be manifested in this place!' The majority of the congregation were not fully aware of what was happening but the leaders immediately knew that she was calling on demonic forces to invade the church. Such confrontations began to increase until we realised that we were in the middle of an intense, spiritual battle.

Many Christians have not yet come to understand the true nature of the battle that confronts us each day of our lives. As children of God it is impossible to live at peace with the devil. And yet, many expect to get on with life as if they were not living in a war zone. Ignorance of the battle is no protection against it.

Behind our visible world with all its apparent physical causes and effects lies a hidden, unseen realm – a spirit world. True opposition comes from a dark, demonic kingdom which is highly organised and dangerous. Satan is its evil head. He is called the prince of this world and the god of this age. Bible teachers are divided concerning how much influence Satan has over the affairs of people in the world, and we do not always know how he operates. But every indication of Scripture is that he has formidable power and he must not be underestimated. The Apostle Paul explains: 'For our struggle is not against flesh and blood but against the rulers, against the authorities, against the powers of this dark world and against the spiritual forces of evil in the heavenly realms' (Ephesians 6:12).

Having said that, Scripture also leaves us in no doubt that Jesus Christ has defeated Satan and all his demonic hordes: 'And having disarmed the powers and authorities, he made a public spectacle of them, triumphing over them by the cross' (Colossians 2:15).

The Church of Jesus Christ is his body and we are called to administer this triumphant victory over Satan. As we engage the enemy in the name of Jesus we press forward the progress of the gospel on the earth.

Needless to say, when this open conflict began we intensified our prayer efforts but we were missing one vital dimension – warfare prayer. Unaware that we had stirred up a hornets' nest we were far too polite in our praying. This was no time to nurture civilian attitudes. We had to arm ourselves and pretty quickly. We were failing to meet the spiritual onslaught of the enemy. Satan is the father of lies, the arch deceiver and full of ferocious aggression. We were being invaded. There were times when we felt completely exposed, intimidated and defiled. In the light of this, our praying was too passive, much too British! We needed help.

God's answer is near at hand

A follower of the Lord must develop sensitivity to the Spirit, for God nearly always works in a completely unexpected way. In our beleaguered situation, help was there all the time, right under our noses.

By now the trickle of African worshippers at KT had become a steady stream. These men and women were used to such demonic confrontations in their own culture. They had no Western inhibitions in the area of the supernatural. Spiritual warfare was second nature to them.

One person who taught us much in those days was Florence. She was a sophisticated Ugandan princess, highly educated, having studied at Oxford University under C. S. Lewis, and she had held government office. During the Idi Amin regime her husband was murdered and she had fled for her life.

Florence arrived in London, penniless. She began working as a church cleaner in KT. Throughout this period of her life she was fully aware that the devil was trying to destroy her Christian faith but, a determined lady, she emerged stronger than ever. Wanting to use her new spiritual strength, she began to intercede first for Kensington Temple leaders and then for the church. Each day Florence would be found praying over every chair as she cleaned it: 'Lord, fill this church; Lord, fill this church.' Over and over again she prayed.

There were people who didn't understand, those who found Florence's behaviour 'eccentric', but she had gone through too much to be easily put off. Spiritual truths were in operation, spiritual keys were finding spiritual doors. Then, events took a dramatic turn.

Wynne Lewis, who had succeeded Eldin Corsie in 1980, encouraged her to keep up her endeavours. A small group of women began to join her every day in the 'prayer room' – a newly built mezzanine room above the main entrance to the church. Unsuspecting weekday visitors were greeted by a torrent of loud prayers and verbal declarations against the works of Satan in Notting Hill Gate as the battle raged in the room directly above their heads. Suspicious characters entering the building for no good reason turned ner-

vously on their heels and made a swift exit. Warfare
prayer had become a daily reality.

The powers of darkness could not ignore this torrent
of triumphant warfare prayer. They retaliated with an
even greater attack on the work of the church. A
number of satanic groups joined together and pitched
their efforts in a concerted attempt to close down the
church through occult power. This resulted in some of
the most dramatic confrontations we had ever experienced. It all took place openly on the streets a few
blocks from the church building.

Who has more power?

Portobello Market is renowned for its unusual antiques.
You can find anything you want, whether it's expensive
or bric-a-brac. It's a multi-racial area that attracts
tourists from all over the world. All Saints Road is also
well known, its name being synonymous with the
underworld, drugs and illegal trades. Almost anything
could be purchased there. Occult practices were thriv-
ing, their wares readily available over the counter.

Every Saturday morning Florence led a small outreach team to the market. There they would stand
among the crowds of people that came to buy a bargain,
preaching the gospel to the passers-by. The team would
often come up against the antagonism of occult practitioners and those who sold occult literature and the
tools of witchcraft. Outraged at this blatant show of evil,
Florence launched her campaign. Her team began to
fast and pray on the streets against what was happening.

Entering one occult shop notorious for the sale of
witchcraft material, Florence was appalled to discover
a large picture portraying the crucifixion of Jesus
displayed prominently on the wall. It depicted Christ

hanging on the cross with a bear's head in place of his own. Under the picture stood a shrine used for the worship of a demon deity. Florence was provoked by this blasphemous ridiculing of the Lord and immediately confronted the two women shopkeepers.

'Why are you doing this to my Lord Jesus?' she demanded indignantly. The women began to laugh and to mock her. Angry and deeply troubled, Florence raised her hand in defiance and spoke in a loud voice, 'Let us see who has more power – your god or the Lord Jesus Christ! I tell you, you will no longer be able to sell your evil here. I close this place down in the name of Jesus!' With that she turned and stormed out, leaving the women laughing hysterically. Within two weeks the shop was closed, never to reopen.

News of these events rapidly spread to many stall-holders and, of course, among the other occult practitioners. The challenges on the street grew fiercer. It was open confrontation, week by week, but God's power was always present and some occultists began to turn to the Lord. One such morning in the early eighties God openly demonstrated his power over evil in a remarkable way, a way which resulted in many believing and committing their lives to Christ.

The team would regularly stand in a certain place that enabled them to minister to the people and yet not seem to be threatening. They would sing, praise God, testify, hand out leaflets and encourage people to turn to the Lord.

Early one Saturday afternoon, the team were busy witnessing, when they became aware that there were more occultists around than usual. They could sense that something was wrong but what it was they didn't know. So they began to pray. Suddenly several women entered the crowd and began a provocative show of power. These witches had come to discredit the Christians' claims about the power of Christ. It was nothing less than a direct demonic challenge of the team's spiritual authority. Moving among the startled crowd, the women were clapping, then blowing and making fire appear in their cupped hands. It was so bizarre and extraordinary that the astonished crowd grew rapidly to several hundred. The police arrived, concerned about what might develop.

Spiritual power is real

Satan is wily, a deceiver and a liar. Was this a skilled and professional deception masquerading as the supernatural? Or was it actually what it was purporting to be – an exhibition of real supernatural power? In occultism there is, undoubtedly, pernicious fraud and simple baloney, whatever kind of snare it takes. There is also genuine power.

In the West the Church needs to reawaken to spiritual reality. Not superstition – reality. The population at large is having its spiritual views of life largely moulded by the media, especially the entertainment industry, the primary job of which is to entertain, not to teach truth. If only we had more people in the media and the arts who could do both. Most of us can recall pictures of occult practitioners popularly portrayed as helpful, caring individuals, providing a social service, helping people to accept death by pointing to the existence of an after-life. Then there are the rather shrewd but likeable spiritual rogues who prey on the simple-minded: charlatans who never mean any real harm past making a quick profit. Lastly, we've all met the image of the satanist, the dangerously unhinged power freak who dominates weaker characters, the villain of countless books and dramas.

These images of lovable, slightly batty geniality and the psychopath in horns running amok for the purposes of a plot, have reduced the spiritual to a fantasy that exists on a screen or between the pages of a book. Something that entertains with little thrills of horror or with amusement or a romantic and misplaced comfort. All this combines to give the impression that the occult is harmless as long as you don't take it too seriously, as long as it all stays just a bit of fun.

There is a major problem with this outlook. The supernatural is very real and doesn't go away just because you don't believe in it. Sooner or later it comes knocking. I speak with the authority of Scripture and with a working experience of spiritual reality when I tell you that Satan's kingdom is real, powerful and well able to use those who are captured by it, whether they be willing or unwitting victims.

Jesus Christ has all power and all authority

The crowds on the street that day were bedazzled by the witches' display. The team, knowing what was at stake, felt out of their depth. They had never seen anything like this before. It was all beyond them. How does one cope with such a confrontation? They knew Satan's power was real but they didn't know what to do. Quietly they prayed. Then, suddenly, Florence sprang into action.

Pushing her way through the crowds, she came face to face with one of the women. Florence began to pray aloud in the name of Jesus and when she took authority over this vulgar display, instantly the woman lost her bizarre ability. The witches were shocked, humiliated and angry. But Florence was undeterred. She and the rest of the team grew very bold and began to preach the gospel to the crowd who were, by now, completely dumbfounded. Like Elijah before Israel's prophets of Baal, they proclaimed the power of the true and living God.

'Jesus Christ has all power and authority! Believe in Jesus not the devil!' Florence thundered.

After the police had dispelled the crowd many people stayed behind to accept Christ. Later, several members of the occult group themselves became convinced Christians, having seen the reality and power of the gospel.

In the months that followed this great victory, Florence and her companions went on to close many occult centres through prayer, fasting and spiritual confrontation. It was as if a powerful, evil force was being pushed back from the entire area. The effect of all this was seen very clearly back in the church. People seemed to come from everywhere, flocking in to find Christ's healing and saving power. Many steeped in all kinds of occult practices were set free.

'How can anyone enter a strong man's house and carry off his possessions unless he first ties up the strong man? Then he can rob his house' (Matthew 12:29). We had learned how to bind the strong man and plunder his goods – the explosion had begun!

2 A Developing Relationship

In Spirit and in truth

The Lord longs to draw men and women to himself, and he has chosen to do it through us, his Church. Wherever God's people have given themselves to earnestly pray and seek him, he has faithfully poured out his grace and his favour. In some parts of the world this has been happening for years. In other places, particularly Europe, we are just beginning to see the Lord moving once more among his Church in revival power. There are now many churches growing in size and spiritual impact in Britain and the rest of Europe.

I believe the Lord wants to gather us, to draw his Church together, to teach us and to lead us. If we are Christians, if we have given our lives to the Lord, then each of us is in a living partnership with Jesus. We are yoked to him. One partner doesn't move without the other. Do you see what I am saying? The Lord will not move without us and we certainly cannot move without him. So what do we do? Are we stuck? And if so, where are we stuck?

Before we can begin to look at prayer there is a fundamental question to be considered. We may say we really want the Lord to speak to us but do we want

to hear him? Are we ready to take him at his Word?
Are we prepared for the reality of this relationship?

I ask this question because the rock of reality is one
on which I believe many of us have foundered.

'I am the way and the truth and the life' (John 14:6).
Most of us will know these words of Jesus well. We all
want the life so we accept the way, but the truth?
Sometimes we shrink back from the truth. The truth is
reality; bare, exposed reality. Reality as God sees it.
Reality comes in all sorts of shades, some of them
warm, comforting and encouraging; others uncomfortable and even exposing, admonishing or warning.

It is a great untruth that Jesus is some kind of polite
Englishman in the sky who only ever speaks nice words.
You only have to look at what he said to the teachers
of religion and Pharisees of his day. He called them
'hypocrites', 'blind guides', 'blind fools', 'sons of hell',
'whitewashed tombs', 'snakes', a 'brood of vipers'.
I don't think the money-changers, the merchants or
the shopping public of the Temple were very keen
on his attitude either. Yet this same Jesus is the truth.
He is telling us that he is reality. But remember, he
is also the way and the life. We cannot travel the
way, we cannot have the life, without also having the
reality.

Everyday Holy Spirit reality

It sometimes takes years for the Holy Spirit to weave
his truth into our lives. This may be because we have
come out of a great darkness that has left us scarred
and in need of healing. Perhaps we have been sheep
without a shepherd and no one has nurtured us in the
faith. We may never have given the Holy Spirit time to
speak to us or to apply Scripture to our hearts. Some-

times we are slow to understand; more often we resist the Spirit's promptings.

It is not enough just to agree intellectually that something is true. We have to digest truth so that it becomes part of our being. We have to be 'truth' full or, to put it another way, we have to be 'in truth'.

Where and when does the Holy Spirit weave truth into the fabric of our lives? Sometimes it takes an unusual incident to enable us to lay hold of God's truth. But it is in the commonplace, everyday experiences of our lives that truth becomes part of us.

Ann was bright, intelligent and attractive. She was superficially happy but felt strangely dissatisfied with her life. Beneath the surface lay a dark reality from which she felt no escape. Hiding the hurts of an abused childhood she made attack her best means of defence. Her husband Tony, not without his own faults, loved her but was constantly kept at arm's length by Ann, who could not accept his affection. Tragically their marriage ended in divorce. It was not until Ann's second marriage was showing the same signs of collapse that she began to face the reality of her pain and the understandable yet destructive strategies she used to cover it. The truth hurt at first, but then it began to bring release as she slowly let go of her pain and drew her security from Christ.

As we choose, like Ann, to follow the Spirit's leadings and elevate him over our own struggles, we grow in spiritual stature and in a strength that is not our own. Truth shines in us brighter and clearer and we find we have developed a great appetite for it.

Why is it so important to love the truth? The Spirit of God longs to lead us into all truth. If we don't love truth there is no way we are going to yield to the one who is truth. Not without a fight, anyway. Perhaps even a lifetime of walking in circles in a barren wilderness.

Stuck in the wilderness

'Then Jesus was led by the Spirit into the desert to be tempted by the devil' (Matthew 4:1).

Jesus followed the Holy Spirit into the wilderness. And so shall we. We may not find ourselves literally in the Sinai or the Sahara but there are times when the circumstances of our lives can seem as relentlessly hard as if we were. We find ourselves tired, weary of the toil of day-to-day experience, exposed to far too much ultra-violet light.

The desert is a parched place, full of life-threatening dangers. When the Israelites travelled through it the Lord meant them to trust him each and every day for food and water. He was their guide by day and night. They could only survive if they depended totally on him.

A whole generation died in that desert. Instead of coming out victoriously into the promised land they perished in the wilderness. Why? For the simple reason that it was a hard journey and they would not yield to their God. They wouldn't believe him. They wouldn't trust him when the going was hard. They didn't want a two-way relationship with the Lord if it meant they had to listen to him, to take note of his words, to bow to his greater understanding of their lives and their situation. It required of them humility and hope and steadfastness in the midst of desolation; a brokenness of the human spirit and a dependence on the Spirit of God.

The Lord provided them with shoes for travelling, with fresh food each day and with water. But the journey was relentless and tiring. The picture in their minds of lush pastures, spring rains, flocks and herds began to fade. They grew impatient. Life was hard, very hard. Was it going to go on like this for ever? They started to resent the journey. Some even thought they had been better off as slaves in Egypt. Where was this land flowing with milk and honey anyway? Where was ease and contentment? All they could see was dry and shifting sand. Does this sound familiar?

Fears got the better of them. They lost faith in their God. If the Lord wouldn't get them out they'd look around for another god who would. As a result of sexual immorality, twenty-three thousand of them died in one day. Some tested God and were killed by snakes. Those who grumbled all the time were killed by the destroying angel. Why were these things written down? Don't you think these people would have preferred to hide their shame? Well, these were God's people just as we are. And their deadly mistakes were written down for our benefit. 'These things happened to them as examples and were written down as warnings for us, on whom the fulfilment of the ages has come' (1 Corinthians 10:11).

God's real agenda

Like the Israelites, we want God's promises. But are we, like them, avoiding his real agenda? Humility, the ability to receive genuine spiritual power from the hand of the Lord, faith, trust, fidelity, love, a dependence on God alone, a spirit sensitive and responsive to God's heart: these are the characteristics that the Lord is seeking to develop in his people. But when it comes down to it, do we insist that God dances to our tune? Do we, like his people of old, turn to grumbling and complaining? Perhaps we elevate our own sense of justice – how could God allow this to happen? Why didn't he give us that? After all, don't we deserve so much more? Some of us stamp our feel like spoilt children. If my Father is the God of the universe then why doesn't he give me what I want?

Do you know that it is possible to spend years in a sulk, having fallen out with one's Father? I don't mean to make light of this situation because the reasons behind it are often far from childish. Grievous and damaging experiences can keep us chained down, preventing us from maturing spiritually. We can either dwell on our pain or we can go on, trusting the creativity of our God and his genuine ability to work all things together for good. Too often that's a cop-out phrase that people use to justify ignoring gross sin or devastating injustice. But there are times when we must trust God, regardless.

I enjoyed a happy boyhood in Africa, the place of my birth, and have many fond memories of our family life. However, my father had to spend long absences from us as work took him away from home, sometimes for quite long periods. His interests were more practical and mechanical and I preferred reading books or doing things which were more creative and artistic in nature. This distancing was to produce later on in life a difficulty in fully understanding how much God was interested in me. But over the years it has been a real joy to discover real intimacy with God, especially in prayer. My childhood hurts now seem trivial by comparison to the warmth and closeness of real fellowship with my heavenly Father.

Do you feel that God has let you down? That you have truly tried your best and it just wasn't good enough for him? If this is the rock that has marooned you in the sea of shifting sand then don't despair. The One who started you on this journey is not about to leave you in the wilderness. Remember, you are yoked together. Take heart. Stop eating sand right now. There is a way out, but it is his way. You have to walk it, leaning on him in humility. Seek him. Listen to him. Start walking.

The wilderness is the place where we find out who we really are. It is a place where reality is made manifest, to us and to the spiritual powers in heavenly realms. It is the place where we, like Jesus, will be sorely tested and, by remaining in him, will learn to defeat both Satan and our own wayward desires. The conflict may be desperate but victory in the wilderness means passage into the promised land.

Jesus went into the desert 'full of the Spirit'. He didn't spend forty years there, as did the children of Israel, but he was there for forty days and forty nights, fasting and praying. It was hard but he was faithful and at the end of that time he walked out 'in the power of the Spirit'. And so can we.

What is prayer?

When we talk about our prayer lives we are talking about something very personal, vital and unique: our relationship with our God. That is why there can be no easy formulas. How can I, or anyone for that matter, tell you exactly how to speak to God? To do that I would have to know all about you and all about God. But there are principles and there are impediments, just as there are in any relationship. We'll go on to look at some of those later, but first let's take a look at what prayer actually is.

Imagine this situation: a newly married couple in love. You can see them doting on each other, can't you, sometimes without words, sometimes talking endlessly? They enjoy spending time in each other's company, in fact they enjoy nothing more. They share each other's lives, appreciating each other, learning how to please each other, delighting to be together, preoccupied with building a joint future.

In such a close and committed relationship communication is as total as the two people involved can make it. Everything is up for discussion. From this foundation of love, trust and security comes the belief that together they can weather any storm the future can hurl at them.

'But Colin,' you may say, 'that's all so idealistic, so ungrounded.' Is it? Many of us are well aware of our partner's human failings yet we enter the relationship with faith, believing that together we can work things through. This is a graphic picture of Christ's relationship with us. Scripture calls the Church the bride of Christ. You and I are, figuratively speaking, Jesus' 'other half' – his bride, his love, his cherished partner.

Let's take a look at another couple. He has just come home from work and is relaxing in his favourite chair, reading the newspaper, his mind on important things: the stock market, the football results, the latest scandal. She may have spent hours cleaning indelible oil marks off the kitchen floor, trodden in the previous day when he walked straight in from the garage. His mind was on important things then, too. The car.

It doesn't take long before his wife begins to feel devalued and used. Perhaps she even starts to believe that her function in life is to run around laying herself down over all the puddles of daily living so that her partner can walk across them without so much as dampening a foot.

And how does he feel? Perhaps he's having a hard time at work. Doesn't she realise how important it is to have the right image? Doesn't she know how draining it is to battle against bosses who don't know what they're doing and then blame you when everything goes wrong? Doesn't she know how many businesses are going to the wall / how hard it would be to get another job / how trapped he feels? Even when he makes a supreme effort and decides to pay her some attention, all she wants to do is go to sleep. She's worn out with the children / work / cleaning the kitchen floor. He begins to feel irrelevant. He might as well be the lodger.

The circumstances of lives differ enormously, of course, but we all know how stress and strain can overtake relationships. A couple who stop making time (and sometimes it has to be 'made') for each other begin to fall prey to all sorts of resentments. They stop sharing their hearts. Each individual is wrapped up in his or her own world, unable to communicate with the other. They begin to grow thick skins and deliberately develop deaf ears in case they actually hear something and then have to muster the effort to respond. Emotions grow cold or hostile.

The logical outcome of this is a marriage where, if the partners stay together at all it is only out of the habit of daily ritual or financial convenience or, perhaps, even cowardice – it's sometimes easier to carry on in apathy than to face up to *reality*, *change* and the *unknown*. People start to live separate lives, full of sadness, bitterness and isolation. A black detachment comes between them; deep disappointment masked by indifference. They end up in separate beds in separate rooms, married in nothing but name.

Our relationship with the Lord can become like that, the only difference being that his desire is always that we come again to him, that we regain our heart communication and begin, once more, to share our lives in a real way. 'Take my yoke upon you and learn from me, for I am gentle and humble in heart, and you will find rest for your souls. For my yoke is easy and

my burden light' (Matthew 11:29–30). We are yoked to
him and he is ready to carry the greater weight but we
have to allow him to do it. We have to receive his
guidance. We have to learn from him. We have to
communicate. He will not drag us along.

Communication – the evidence of relationship

Non-communication grieves the Spirit of God just as
you would be grieved if your partner, for whom you
had sacrificed everything, constantly cold-shouldered
you or found almost everything else more important or
desirable than spending time with you. Jesus says:

> I am the vine; you are the branches. If a man remains
> in me and I in him, he will bear much fruit; apart
> from me you can do nothing. If anyone does not
> remain in me, he is like a branch that is thrown away
> and withers; such branches are picked up, thrown
> into the fire and burned. If you remain in me and my
> words remain in you, ask whatever you wish, and it
> will be given you. (John 15:5–7).

Now let's look at this carefully. If we have no prayer
life at all, if we are not communicating with Jesus,
how can we claim to be in Christ, the vine? Jesus
says we are 'like a branch that is thrown away and
withers'. Our relationship has become like that couple
who live separate lives, joined in name only. And
what will become of us? We will be 'picked up, thrown
into the fire and burned'. It won't matter how many
excuses we make for ourselves, how many good works
we have done or how much pleading we indulge in.
Jesus says:

Not everyone who says to me 'Lord, Lord,' will enter the kingdom of heaven, but only he who does the will of my Father who is in heaven. Many will say to me on that day, 'Lord, Lord, did we not prophesy in your name, and in your name drive out demons and perform many miracles?' Then I will tell them plainly, 'I never knew you. Away from me, you evildoers!' (Matthew 7:21–3).

So, you can see it is very important that we are doing the will of the Father. And how can we know if we are? By asking him. By listening to his words. By learning how to communicate with him. By staying 'in the vine'.

Perhaps we are still speaking to the Lord but have stopped sharing our hearts. It is possible to say a great deal, to speak mountains of words, and to communicate nothing. We can even prevent communication by using words. Many more people 'say prayers' than ever truly pray. Are we simply more interested in other things? Perhaps we are centred more on ourselves than in the vine? If this is the case we are spiritually withering and in danger of ending up on the fire.

If sin has come between us and the Lord then we need to know, we need to look at our mistakes and learn from them so that they are not repeated. He will never turn us away. Remember the parable of the prodigal son? Regardless of how far we have fallen we can turn from our sin and come back to the Lord. He will not only forgive us, he will run to meet us. We can find again that heart relationship, we can still be part of the vine and, perhaps, a wiser part at that. You can start again whether you are nine or ninety. It is never too early or too late.

Intimacy in relationship

What is the relationship, then, that Jesus wants to have with us, his bride? It is one of intimacy, letting nothing come between us so that we can say with Paul:

> For I am convinced that neither death nor life, neither angels nor demons, neither the present nor the future, nor any powers, neither height nor depth, nor anything else in all creation, will be able to separate us from the love of God that is in Christ Jesus our Lord (Romans 8:38–9).

Prayer is real communication, the manifestation of intimacy with our God. In an intimate relationship a couple are constantly learning about each other, sharing their heart attitudes. We, the bride, will be eager to learn more about the partner to whom we are yoked. Christ is our husband, master, king, saviour, redeemer, friend ... the list goes on and on. Through him we have access to a righteous and good heavenly Father who has put our past sins as far away from us as east is from west.

'But,' you may say, 'didn't Jesus leave us? Didn't he return to the Father? Why did he do that?' Jesus explained that if he didn't go, the Holy Spirit wouldn't come. 'But I tell you the truth: it is for your good that I am going away. Unless I go away, the Counsellor will not come to you; but if I go, I will send him to you' (John 16:7).

Jesus, though the Son of God and of a divine nature, was also man. As the 'Son of man', he is like us and understands us completely. Now Jesus, being man, cannot be physically present everywhere at once, just as we cannot. But the Holy Spirit can be anywhere and everywhere he is sent. Jesus returned to the Father so that the Holy Spirit could come to us, each of us, and indwell us.

Total communication for all of us

> When he, the Spirit of truth, comes, he will guide you into all truth. He will not speak on his own; he will speak only what he hears, and he will tell you what is yet to come. He will bring glory to me by taking from what is mine and making it known to you. All that belongs to the Father is mine. That is why I said the Spirit will take from what is mine and make it known to you (John 16:13–15).

Jesus said that the Spirit would take what was his own and give it to us, collectively. When we pray we have total communication with God: Father, Son and Holy Spirit, and he has total communication with us.

So to meet with our Lord is easy – his Holy Spirit lives inside us. Wherever we are, there he is also. We, who have given our lives to him, have already entered into an intimate relationship. Now we have to nurture it, to strengthen it, to learn more about our Lord, to listen to his instructions, to allow our God to deepen this holy, exciting and fulfilling partnership. And this is for all of us. For you and for me.

We have to stop seeing prayer as the exclusive province of the minister or the vicar or the pastor or the parish priest or the intercession group or the convent or that weird little group round the corner. It is something that deeply involves you and deeply involves me. It is the very lifeblood of our relationship with Jesus. It is total two-way communication with our God. And that's power!

The blight of 'worm-consciousness'

Prayer is powerful! So powerful that, were we to begin to catch a glimpse of this truth, we would indeed pray without ceasing. Is it any wonder, then, that anything and everything rises up to distract and deflect us? Sometimes these unwelcome diversions are part of our circumstances, sometimes they are from within us, the result of anxieties or a crippling lack of self-esteem. It is the latter that I want us to examine now.

We are back to our picture of the young bride and her new husband. The husband comes in at the door and there she is, the woman he has chosen for himself. He looks fondly at her. What does she do? Does she run to meet him with a kiss? No. Does she put the kettle on and tell him about her day? No. This is what she does. She crawls up to his feet.

'Don't look at me,' she says, cowering on the floor, 'my dress is dirty and full of holes from crawling around. Don't look at my hair; it's awful. Oh, I'm too fat; turn your head away. Oh, I'm so boring; I know you won't want to listen to my prattling conversation. I've got nothing to say that's worthy enough for your ears. Oh, it's so painful for me to meet you like this. You can't possibly want to see me and I know I can't live up to what you want me to be. Let's stop meeting. If I have to speak to you I can always pass a note on through someone else who's much more acceptable than me.'

Can you see how frustrated and sad that poor man would be? He has chosen his bride because he wants her, he loves her. In his eyes she is lovely, attractive in every way, like a fresh bud closed up tight which would, if it opened out, release its full potential: joy, freshness, creativity, captivating colours, a delightful scent. But what is she doing to herself?

It is a ridiculous situation and, were you or I to see it happening in real life, we would have no hesitation in sending in a psychiatrist and/or praying and fasting for the poor woman's deliverance. Yet this very same scenario is acted out over and over again in our churches and, somehow, we've come to accept it as normal. How far from reality we've slid!

One dear woman I remember used to approach God with this mentality. Her prayers were usually offered while she was wallowing in self-deprecation. She spent so much time talking about her own unworthiness that she forgot the worthiness of Jesus. Needless to say, she received very few answers to prayer. In fact she hardly ever asked God specifically for anything. She was too preoccupied with her unworthiness to receive. But the Bible teaches us to focus on Christ and his worth and not on ourselves and our failings.

'Worm-consciousness' in the bride of Christ has nothing to do with Christianity; it is totally anti-gospel. It isn't meekness, it isn't spirituality, it isn't humility. Yes, once we were dead in our sins; metaphorically speaking we were dressed in rags, lost and unlovely. But we have come to Christ! We have been washed, cleansed, forgiven, reborn of the Spirit of God. Even if we fall into sin all is not lost. We can repent, put right that which can be repaired, know forgiveness and be restored. To keep reliving the bad old days, to immerse oneself in memories of old sins is not only perverse and likely to keep us in their grip but it is living in denial of what Christ has done for us.

A new creation

Deeper problems may need ministry, counselling, some therapy or a combination of these. Some changes happen in us overnight but many, many others happen gradually as we listen to and obey the voice of the Holy Spirit.

Spiritual growth takes time, travelling through a wilderness takes time, running a race takes time. We must guard against being impatient with ourselves, each other and our God. He is the author and the perfecter of our faith. What matters is that we follow him, that we are constantly moving forward, that we start to lay hold of his promises.

We are a new creation, growing and opening out. Our God wants to change us from glory into glory. We are urged: 'Throw off everything that hinders and the sin that so easily entangles, and let us run with perseverance the race marked out for us' (Hebrews 12:1).

Scripture teaches us that God has 'raised us up with Christ and seated us with him in the heavenly realms' (Ephesians 2:6), that we are capable of being 'filled to the measure of all the fulness of God' (Ephesians 3:19), that we 'will judge angels' (1 Corinthians 6:3). So let's see this 'worm consciousness' for what it is – a satanic lie designed to keep us apart from the Lord, cowed and in condemnation and, most importantly, powerless – unable to pray with the boldness and creativity that is our inheritance in Christ.

Rather, let us begin to open up to God, knowing his love accepts us totally. From this base we can begin to grow in our relationship with God and a natural part of that will be prayer. We will not be just saying prayers but actually talking with our heavenly Father. We will be sharing heart to heart in two-way communion: God sharing his love with us, while we respond in love to him.

3 Where are the Elijahs?

Power with God

I once heard of a brother in the Lord who, having experienced the reality of the Holy Spirit, went immediately to the nearest hospital, certain that the Lord would heal everyone in it. He laid his hands on the first patient he saw, a man in a wheelchair, and prayed for healing. He demanded it. He jumped and declared it. Nothing happened. The poor man was not healed; the brother went home angry and dejected.

Alone in his room he berated the Lord. 'Where is the God of Elijah?' he roared. Imagine his amazement when the Lord replied, 'Where are the Elijahs?'

And there's the nub of the problem. Where *are* the Elijahs? Are they cowering in caves? Have they been driven into hiding? Have they been prevented from maturing? Perhaps they are wandering somewhere in the wilderness? I believe the Lord wants to open our eyes, to give us a clarity of vision, a new understanding of the secret of power with God.

Elijah was one of the most powerful of all the Old Testament prophets. He called fire from heaven, raised the dead and confronted the backslidden nation of Israel. And the secret of his power was prayer. Even the word God gave him for the nation had to be prayed over before it was released to become effective. In the first book of Kings we read of him declaring God's judgement that there would be no rain for a season, but the fuller picture emerges from the New Testament: Elijah had to pray effectively in order to see it happen. 'The prayer of a righteous man is powerful and effective. Elijah was a man just like us. He prayed earnestly that it would not rain, and it did not rain on the land for three and a half years. Again he prayed, and the heavens gave rain, and the earth produced its crops' (James 5:16–18).

How can we experience God's power like Elijah? From these verses of Scripture we can glean exactly what is needed. If we look at verse 16 in several translations, the meaning becomes very clear:

'The prayer of the righteous is powerful and effective' (NRSV).

'The earnest (heartfelt, continued) prayer of a righteous man makes tremendous power available [dynamic in its working]' (Amplified Bible).

'The effective, fervent prayer of a righteous man avails much' (NKJV).

'Effective prayer of a righteous man can accomplish much' (NASV)

'Prayer of a righteous man has great power in its effects' (RSV).

'The earnest prayer of a righteous man has great power and wonderful results' (Living Bible paraphrase).

Now the Greek dynamic equivalent:

'Prayer fervently made by a righteous person, arising out of a felt need and as the result of the working of God, has great power to effect change.'

This verse is not just about prayer. It is about powerful, effective prayer which, we are told, is fervent. Wherever God is moving powerfully in the world, without exception you also find fervent prayer. I have in my possession a most inspiring video recorded in the underground church of China. It is 5.00 a.m. and the people have gathered for two hours of special prayer. A visiting preacher from the West is present, waiting to give some much needed encouragement to these brave believers suffering under the heavy hand of persecution.

The video shows these people deep in prayer, and so fervent are their efforts that you immediately assume that they must be praying for some obvious need such as their safety or protection. From the old to the very young – all are engrossed in prayer. Minute by minute the intensity grows even stronger. There is no 'polite' praying in turn. Instead everyone is calling on God out loud and at once, each one intensely engaging him for themselves, and yet at the same time, somehow remaining in concert with each other. It barely seems possible, but the praying grows even stronger still, but there is not even a hint of extremism or loss of control. Some are standing lifting their arms towards heaven. Others are kneeling with their hands clasped earnestly together. Many are prostrate. Many are weeping as they pray. Then you hear the reason for all this prayer: these people are not praying for themselves, but for the preacher – that God will bless his message. No wonder there is revival in China today!

Fervent prayer does not involve having to work yourself up into some kind of frenzied emotional state before God will answer. Fervency is the result of identification with a felt need and a determination to see that need answered.

There are two Greek words for prayer: *proseuche* stressing dependence on God and *deesis* which emphasises the need, the reason why you are praying. In this verse prayer is described by the word *deesis*. The Holy

Spirit is revealing the principle that effective prayers arise out of a sense of need.

We all know how to pray when we need to, don't we! Take the story of one woman, for example. Marie was just about to leave for work, when there was a telephone call from school: 'Lucy's had an accident! She is on the way to hospital.' The information was scant and Marie had no idea how seriously injured her daughter was. A cold, sickening feeling grabbed her inside and, numb with shock, she drove furiously to the hospital. 'Oh God!' she cried out, again and again. It was instinctive, coming from deep within. She was desperate, but she was praying and God was listening.

Marie did not have to be taught how to identify with this need in prayer. Neither did she have to try hard to work up a fervent prayer. If we allow him the Holy Spirit can help us to feel another individual's or nation's need as personally and strongly as she felt the need of her child. In intercession we enter into other people's needs as if they were our own. But more of this later.

Deal with unrighteousness

The principle that you cannot live defectively and pray effectively is a crucial one. We cannot pray powerfully if we are living in unrighteousness. It is a simple fact of Scripture and life. 'Surely the arm of the Lord is not too short to save, nor his ear too dull to hear. But your iniquities have separated you from God; your sins have hidden his face from you, so that he will not hear' (Isaiah 59:1–2).

Unrighteousness stops the work of the Holy Spirit. We cannot pray to God from a distance, shouting our requests across a chasm. If we have sinned then we need to confess our failures honestly and turn right round from them. We can ask the Holy Spirit to strengthen us and enable us to continue our journey. We are not perfect creatures; it is inevitable that we shall find shortcomings in ourselves. And if we don't the Holy Spirit will point them out to us! This is good, right and appropriate. It is all part of God's work within us as he changes us into the likeness of his Son.

Jesus understands this and was at pains to teach it to his disciples. Remember how put out Peter was when Jesus wanted to wash his feet? He thought it just wasn't appropriate. Here are Jesus' thoughts on the subject:

'No,' said Peter, 'you shall never wash my feet.'

Jesus answered, 'Unless I wash you, you have no part with me.'

And again:

'Jesus answered, "A person who has had a bath needs only to wash his feet; his whole body is clean. And you are clean . . . "' (John 13:8–10).

Having owned and confessed our sin, the Lord can wash our feet; he cleanses us and forgives us. The matter is over, dealt with. There is no reason to get stuck, but sometimes we do get stuck.

Sin and guilt

Unrighteousness presents us with two traps. The first, which we have already touched on, is condemnation. This is the voice of the accuser who loves to whisper (and sometimes to shout) that we're just not worthy enough. 'Why would God ever listen to you? You let him down so often.' Remember, the prayer of a righteous person has great power in its effects, so our spiritual adversary will try to stop us before we even begin. We need to remind him and ourselves that we've already had our bath! The blood of Jesus has taken away our sin. Jesus is our righteousness and we come to God through grace not by works; we claim our inheritance through his grace towards us not through our startlingly wonderful performance. Thankfully!

All we then need to do is come to the Lord and present our feet! Many people lack confidence in prayer because they lack assurance of their salvation and forgiveness. The good news of the gospel is that, in Christ, both are ours! 'Dear friends, if our hearts do not condemn us, we have confidence before God and receive from him anything we ask, because we obey his commands and do what pleases him' (1 John 3:21–2).

Dishonesty in the inward parts

God certainly isn't waiting for us to become perfect before we communicate with him. What he does require, however, are hearts that do not hold on to or 'cherish' sin. Which brings me to the second trap of unrighteousness – cherishing sin.

'If I had cherished sin in my heart, the Lord would not have listened' (Psalm 66:18).

What is this cherishing of sin? The obvious answer is deliberately holding on to a sin and not giving it up; quite wilfully deciding that you'll do what you like whatever the Lord may think about it. It may be some secret attraction you are cherishing rather than rejecting. Or it could be one of a whole range of negative emotions and reactions that we have to guard against: anger, resentment, criticism or prejudice. Often it is the thing that we fail to do that we know we should be doing: giving quality time to those close to us, defending the truth or standing up for the right. Deliberately holding onto sins like these despite warnings from the

Lord will count against your prayer life. It is an obvious rebellion and leads to circling in the wilderness, where the rebellious heart perishes or undergoes immense struggles until it yields.

There is, of course, the softer version which is just as rebellious but more quietly so. This is how it goes: 'I'll let you be Lord of my life, well, most of my life, anyway, but you've got to let me keep that little bit, I enjoy it so much. I really feel much better for it.' Or more deceitfully, 'I can serve you better if you let me keep it.' This also leads to an extended spell of sand-bathing. You can never bargain with the Lord over sin. Give it up! You'll lose something that is destroying and disempowering you and you'll experience a fuller measure of the Spirit of God, confidence and power in prayer.

The less obvious, but equally damaging, way of cherishing sin is by not quite admitting to yourself that it *is* sin in the first place, in other words, turning a deaf ear to the Holy Spirit.

Rejecting our sin

Sometimes we are complacent. We think that God accepts us anyway. What's a little sin here and there? After all, it's not that big; it's just a shadow. That puts us in the position of refusing to let Jesus wash our feet. But remember what Jesus said to Peter, 'Unless I wash you, you have no part with me.'

Repentance doesn't mean being sorry, although that has its place. Neither does it mean admitting to and confessing a sin, though that too has its place. Repentance means, more fundamentally, turning away from sin.

When we come to the Lord and turn from our sin

then the Holy Spirit will require all sorts of things of us, things such as apologising to someone, or maybe even many people. We will have to do our best to put right a wrong we have inflicted. It might even seem humiliating. How could the Spirit of God want us to feel so terrible?

I have deliberately used the word 'humiliating' here because it is often how people in such a situation feel. The feeling is, however, just a symptom of the problem. Backtracking over our behaviour with others, apologising and making restoration is not humiliating but it is humbling. It can also be healing and releasing, both to the offender and the offended against. Most of all it gladdens Jesus, who prayed that we 'all may be one'. Of course, there are instances where backtracking of this sort may be unhelpful, but let the Spirit judge and tell you. Such instances are very, very rare.

Our response to the Holy Spirit can take six seconds or six decades. Why waste precious time going round and round the wilderness? It's no good being extremely fervent and praying over issues with tears and fasting: if you are cherishing sin in your life, God will not hear. '*If* my people, who are called by my Name, will *humble themselves*, and *pray*, and *seek my face* and *turn* from their wicked ways, *then I will hear* from heaven and *will forgive* their sin and *will heal* their land' (2 Chronicles 7:14).

'Forgive us our debts as ...'

The Lord's prayer includes this sentence: 'Forgive us our debts as we also have forgiven our debtors' (Matthew 6:12). Verses 14 and 15 go on to tell us: 'If you forgive men when they sin against you, your heavenly Father will also forgive you. But if you do not forgive men their sins, your Father will not forgive your sins.'

Sin, as we have seen, cuts us off from God. As much as he loves us he cannot and will not ignore it. He is just and perfect and can only accept us because of Jesus' perfect sacrifice. And it is justice that is at the root of this statement. Is it just that our God should forgive us every weakness, every shortfall so that we can then go and self-righteously hold the sins of others against them? We are nothing ourselves without God's grace – what gives any of us the right to nurse grievances and give the devil a foothold?

Unforgiveness is one of the deadliest obstacles to prayer. We will all know times, even though it may be very hard, when we have to forgive our enemies, to leave the righteousness of our cause with God, to let him dispense justice his way. Moving forward in him leaves us no choice. We must let him be our shield – then we shall live in the freedom and release of the Holy Spirit and the companionship of God instead of spending our days unfulfilled, in a dry and corrosive prison of bitter self-righteousness.

Enter the realm of spiritual reality

Prayer is meant to be put into operation. Elijah learned that well enough. How far would he have developed his calling without prayer? How much would he have experienced God's if he had not developed a life of prayer?

It's not enough just to believe in the power of prayer as a principle or theory – to change anything you actually have to pray! There is another side to this operation too though. When you pray you are caught up in the activity of the Holy Spirit. Part of the equation is human, part divine.

You might say, 'Why do I need to pray? God created the universe. He sustains it. What more can I add? Surely God can do anything he wants to. He doesn't need me.'

It may seem a logical argument to you but the Lord doesn't always conform to our logic. He has chosen to seat us in heavenly places with Christ; he has chosen to bestow on us the great joy and enormous responsibility of power as we live and move and have our being in him. The way through this complex question is to realise that our arguments are fairly redundant here. We have left the realm of philosophical theories and entered the realm of spiritual reality. God has chosen to include us in bringing about his purposes. Who are we to argue?

'Prayer is the slender nerve that moves the muscles of omnipotence,' says Charles Spurgeon. Another way to put it is: 'Without God we cannot, without prayer he will not.' Our prayers are vital.

You may have a wonderful vacuum cleaner that can do all sorts of things: shampoo, clean and polish. And you may have an electricity supply that will set it in motion, but until you actually get up and switch it on, nothing will happen. You will sit in your room as the dust and cat hairs, fluff and crumbs rise around you, staring in frustration at this switch, powerful but totally non-functional domestic appliance. You will get frustrated. You might even give it an angry kick or verbally abuse its apparent lack of interest.

Now, I am not trying to suggest that God is in any way like a hoover. What I am saying is that he requires our co-operation. That is the spiritual reality. All the philosophy in the world won't turn on that vacuum cleaner. We can look at circuit diagrams, we can debate whether or not its colour matches the decor, we can get experts in to take it to bits, check it over and reassemble it. We can sit for hours, concentrating on it, willing it to move until we can't stand the dirt or the inactivity any more. Then what do we do? We get out a dustpan and brush and, seeing the size of the problem, ring round a few friends. It takes hours. We suffer rota phobia. The results are short lived: the dust begins collecting again as soon as we stop. We are worn out and caught on a do-it-yourself treadmill. This is what happens to a life or a church that is limping along through lack of prayer.

The effective and working operation of God

There are two Greek words for God's power. The first is *dunamis* which means 'inherent might; potential power'. From *dunamis* we get our word 'dynamite'. The second Greek word for God's working power is *energeia* which means 'energise; active power in operation'. We could interpret this as the explosion of the dynamite.

Dunamis is potential power. The power is not yet in operation, like the motionless vacuum cleaner. But as you flick the switch to the 'on' position *energeia*, the released power, starts to flow and the machine leaps into life.

Prayer is like the action of flicking the switch. It is power (*energeia*) in operation. This is why the devil hates it and works so hard to prevent it – he is actually powerless against it. Prayer is the effective and working operation of God. You only experience its power when you pray just as you only experience the power of that vacuum cleaner when you flick the switch to the 'on' position. If you want God's power to be released you have to pray. As powerful as God is, if you don't pray, his power is not released.

True prayer is 'in the Spirit', that is, by the operation of God. When we pray God's power is released because he himself is at work. He has caused us to pray. It isn't that he is ready or waiting to move when we pray – he actually is moving in our prayer. We must not say prayers, we must pray. Prayer should be our spiritual norm. We are born of the Spirit and shouldn't be conscious of the Spirit one day and not the next. 'And pray in the Spirit on all occasions with all kinds of prayers and requests. With this in mind, be alert and always keep on praying for all the saints' (Ephesians 6:18).

Without powerful prayer nothing will change. We are sitting on dynamite but without prayer the explosion never happens. God has given us every potential blessing in Christ and does not withhold anything from us. 'He who did not spare his own Son, but gave him up for us all . . . how will he not also, along with him, graciously give us all things?' (Romans 8:32).

Yet we fail to ask and therefore we fail to receive from God (James 4:2). Many Christians sit on the vast storehouse of God's treasures, his infinite provision and divine opportunities for their lives, but through prayerlessness fail to realise them. The Old Testament shows that Elijah made a great pronouncement confronting the nation of Israel and her rejection of the one true God in favour of pagan idols. 'Now Elijah the Tishbite, from Tishbe in Gilead, said to Ahab, "As the Lord, the God of Israel, lives, whom I serve, there will be neither dew nor rain in the next few years except at my word"' (1 Kings 17:1).

What was the source of Elijah's confidence when he made that bold statement? Was it his prophetic calling? His capacity to hear and speak the words of God? Like that brother who fruitlessly 'pronounced' healing on the wheelchair patient in hospital, Elijah might have shouted himself hoarse and it would have no effect on the weather. The New Testament shows that the real power behind his pronouncement came from prayer. 'Elijah was a man just like us. He prayed earnestly that it would not rain, and it did not rain on the land for three and a half years' (James 5:17).

In the same way all the prophets were also great intercessors. You cannot truly hear the word of God and speak that word out to others without also becoming deeply involved in the outworking of it by prayer. Today we have many people in the Church who are fine speakers and there is no shortage of those who can tell us what we should be doing. Some even do it with fine-sounding prophetic statements. However, there is a desperate shortage of those who can match their impressive words with the powerful prayer that brings them about. Unless we change all that and learn the power of prayer, we will never know the release of God's power. We will fail to impact the world with the effective operation of God. All we will be left with is a glimpse of what might have been possible had we prayed.

When God's will is not released into situations, lives are overtaken by depression, hurt, anger and fatalism. Our churches can be caught up in strife; we try to achieve things for God in our own strength. When things don't work out we can respond by rationalisation and denial, not even acknowledging the fact that we were wrong.

This is a road far from the way of holiness that Isaiah speaks of (Isaiah 35:8). It is neither the way, the truth nor the life. Instead it is a many-laned, barren circuit in a spiritual wilderness of disillusionment, discouragement and unbelief.

Let's determine to stay in the vine, to make our relationship with the Lord our number-one priority, praying on all occasions. And let's see how many 'Elijahs' he gives us!

4 Who Wants to Go to a Boring Prayer Meeting?

God's nightmare and ours

In the last chapter we looked at some of the things that can weaken our relationship with the Lord and, consequently, disempower our prayer lives. It goes without saying that if we are withering individually then when we come together all we are doing is presenting our God with a bumper bundle of dead and dying wood just waiting for the axe. You've got to be either living in gross unreality or harbouring a streak of masochism to admit to actually enjoying a spiritless prayer meeting. It can be drudgery of the worst kind for us and an affront to our God.

A nightmare prayer meeting is one in which the Holy Spirit has been or is being quenched in individual people's hearts. Somehow the whole is more awful than the sum of the parts. This kind of meeting comes in various forms and it often happens when a group of people are reduced to meeting out of duty; their inner motives for getting together may not actually have much to do with prayer at all.

There is the cliquey women's gossip meeting which tags on a few prayers at the end to try and give it a semblance of respectability. There is the men's 'good guy, pillar of society' meeting which is full of criticism and berating of the state of society, this TV programme, that scandal; an 'ain't it awful' moan session that prays self-righteously, stiffly, drily and judgementally.

I won't stay in a 'God-less' prayer meeting. Time is too precious to waste. I'll either leave or do something to radically change it.

Some of the worst meetings I've ever suffered have been very long and arduous, back-breaking in fact, in cold rooms with hard chairs. You get those extended periods of silence, not the silence of contemplation in the presence of God (we shouldn't be frightened of that; in silence the Lord can communicate deeply with us); no, this is the silence of nothing happening.

There is usually only one way of praying, people standing up or praying in turn, and you find people using that as an opportunity to show off in their knowledge of the Scriptures or their incredible spirituality (flowery language that puts other people off praying). There is no direction, no sense that we are engaging God at all.

Making progress in prayer

When we pray we should start at a point and pray through to another point and know that there's a difference between them. We may think there's a lot further to go. We may say, 'We've got to pray more to get through on that one,' but we have to feel that we've made progress. And it doesn't help if the whole meeting is disjointed with different subjects.

For example, the pastor might say, 'Now we're going to pray for the crusade that's happening in a month's time.' And then one lady stands up and says, 'Lord, bless the church and bless the deacons,' 'Dear Lord' this and 'Dear Lord' that. And somebody prays out about Grandma's ingrowing toenails. It isn't that God doesn't care about those things but there's no direction.

In this kind of meeting, at the end of the day, we're going nowhere; nothing is being built up in prayer. There's no leadership, no direction, no spiritual engagement, no sense of the Lord's presence, no sense of listening to God. There isn't any real horizontal contact either; there's no heart-to-heart sharing.

The threat of change

The meeting I have just described is characterised by rigidity and powerlessness. When we allow the Holy Spirit to lead us we have to let go of our preconceived ideas, perhaps baggage that has been with us for many years. We have to be immersed in the Lord and not in ourselves. Scripture speaks of the Holy Spirit in terms of oil, water, wind and fire. We have to allow him to be himself with us, to water us, to blow us where he wills, to warm us, to ignite us, to oil us, to make us supple and responsive to the heart of God.

People tend not to like change. We like the familiar, we like to know where we are, we like to know what to expect and we don't like being embarrassed by finding ourselves unprepared in unfamiliar situations. Change challenges our pride, it stirs up our insecurities and lays bare all sorts of fears. And there's a good side to that. If we have fears that are holding us back then they need to be exposed so that we can seek the Lord's help in dealing with them. And perhaps we have questions and some sensible reservations that have to be consciously explored. But we must always allow God to be God! He will be what he will be.

We have a Father in heaven who upholds the mightiest of principles, the strongest of laws; laws that keep the universe in place, rules without which our world and everything in it would disintegrate. He is a God of order, of pattern, of authority and reliability; he is all those things that make us feel safe and secure. We know this is true. But he is also a God of infinite variety, a creative, spontaneous God, a Spirit of fresh and new life who understands us better than we understand ourselves and still says, 'Move on!'

Our God is always wanting to lead us forward into new territory, just as he longed to lead the Israelites out of the desert and into the promised land all those years ago. And remember, if you stay still in the desert for very long, you die.

They all ate the same spiritual food and drank the same spiritual drink; for they drank from the spiritual rock that accompanied them, and that rock was Christ. Nevertheless, God was not pleased with most of them; their bodies were scattered over the desert (1 Corinthians 10:3–5).

This, my dear brothers and sisters, was written for us! We have a strong God, a God we can trust. Let's rely on the Holy Spirit, allowing him to free us, to lead us and to move us on into the adventure of truly Spirit-led prayer.

Which of you fathers, if your son asks for a fish, will give him a snake instead? Or if he asks for an egg will give him a scorpion? If you then, though you are evil, know how to give good gifts to your children, how much more will your Father in heaven give the Holy Spirit to those who ask him! (Luke 11:11–13).

When we are living deep in the vine, feeding on Jesus' overwhelming love for us, then we are freed to walk in his Spirit, acting out of his love and not imprisoned by our own insecurities.

Let's not mistake rigidity for security and earthly conformity for obedience to God. Let's hold fast to every good thing, every past truth given to us by the Holy Spirit. But let's let him be God of the present too, touching us in unique ways because we are unique people. In the company of such a creative and loving Spirit, how can life be dull? How can prayer meetings be boring?

We are the Church

Our individual prayer lives are not lived in the isolation we sometimes think they are. True, each of us has a very personal relationship with Christ, our bridegroom, but we influence each other too.

To the extent that the members of a church have set out their tents and made their home in the wilderness then that church is stuck; it won't matter how charismatic the leader is – he'll soon suffer burn-out or be given his marching orders! If the leadership of a church is stuck then the members will be stuck too. They may stay for a while, out of loyalty or hope that something will change, but if the leadership refuses to move forward in the Spirit then every bit of life in the church will either be chased out or flogged to death.

The way we work together as a church is compared in Scripture to the working of a body. Christ is the head; it is he who plans, who co-ordinates, who originates and supervises our movements. We are the myriad different parts: all the pieces that form the rest of the body – hands, feet, limbs, internal organs, senses.

When we are joined to the head, which is Christ, then not only are we being sustained, we are being directed in different ways; we become increasingly aware of our true identity in Christ. When we carry out those tasks he has put on our hearts, we are doing so in harmony with the rest of the body. The head isn't going to direct the left foot to run left and the right foot to run right!

What happens when different parts of the body become detached from the head? The answer is simple: they die. If they are not already severed they soon will be. Gangrene sets in, and gangrene, if not cut out, is capable of destroying the whole body.

I have seen the consequences of this in church life. Wherever people do not hold firmly to Christ the head, there is confusion and chaos. One young member of our church felt 'called to evangelise' and did indeed have a great deal to offer in this area. But instead of consulting with his leaders and spending time preparing for his ministry, he went out and set up his own organisation. Years later he was still struggling to be really effective in his work for God, and he had left behind him a trail of spiritual casualties as a result of his proud and impulsive actions.

Any body part that is not properly attached to the head cannot function in a healthy way. At best it is suffering partial paralysis. It cannot work in harmony with the rest of the body parts and causes all sorts of damage in the tissues around it. Some tissues might find themselves working extra hard to defend the rest of the body against its failure, then they, too, collapse under the strain. Others may find themselves redundant because there is no working organ to receive that which they were designed to deliver. Limbs begin to atrophy and, gradually, large parts of the body begin to seize up.

A church where the people or the leadership or both are not wholly immersed in Christ is a body trying to exist without a head. Now, do we really want to become zombies? The walking undead? We have a choice before us. It's all or nothing. 'I know your deeds, that you are neither cold nor hot. I wish you were either one or the other! So, because you are lukewarm – neither hot nor cold – I am about to spit you out of my mouth' (Revelation 3:15–16).

We either belong to God or we don't. There's no middle way. We can't say to the bridegroom, 'Oh, I promised myself to you back there, on that date. So I am yours really even though I spend most of my time thinking about other things.' You can't fool the Spirit of God with semantics. He sees truth absolutely.

How attractive is a sleazy bride?

A bride's relationship with a bridegroom is an exclusive one. The very same is true of our relationship with Jesus. We are repeatedly told in the Old Testament that our God is a jealous God. He is Spirit and he has emotions. He feels. We are very similar, made in his likeness. We have a spirit and we feel.

Jealousy is generally seen as a nasty, vengeful and spiteful emotion. The world would have us be more 'reasonable' about our emotions. Being 'reasonable' unfortunately so often means denying what we feel, putting on an acceptable face. But our emotions are real, they are an enormous part of us even as they are an enormous part of our God. Nowhere in Scripture are we asked to deny our emotions. It is never wrong to feel, but it is always wrong to sin.

When we are walking in the Spirit of God we are to subject all our emotions to the Spirit. He is the one who can give us the wisdom and the self-control to deal with strong feelings. And sometimes he even has to do the opposite: liberate our feelings, enable us to feel again! 'In your anger do not sin' (Ephesians 4:26).

Jealousy is often confused with covetousness and envy. We are not to lust after things which do not belong to us whether they be material objects or relationships. The word 'jealousy' is sometimes used instead of 'envy', but jealousy has another meaning: it is the painful emotional reaction of having love stolen away. Sometimes the 'stealing' is more in our own heads than in reality. But there are times when jealousy is a very appropriate reaction.

Let's go back to our picture. Can you imagine the feelings of a bridegroom whose bride spends every other night with someone else round the corner, and then, on alternate weekends, visits an old flame for a bit of rekindling? How would this bridegroom react do you think? Would he say, 'Oh well, that's all right just as long as you visit me every other Thursday'? Or, 'You stay with him for six months and then spend six months with me'? Of course not.

Our relationship with our God is an exclusive one. We must not share that unique union with anyone or anything else. Our God alone must be our guide and our truest love. Nothing, absolutely nothing, must edge between the bride and the bridegroom.

The Lord knows our needs. He longs to bless us with good things, good relationships. He will but we must take care never to elevate any thing or relationship above that which we have with him. And that goes for family members and church leaders too. No one, nothing, must mean more to us than our God.

Spiritual idolatry

This position of putting someone or something in a higher place in our heart than God is called idolatry. The Lord will require us to give up whatever is blocking our relationship with him. He knows and loves us so much, however, that if we willingly surrender the thing to him he will often give it back to us. Sometimes it's just a matter of getting our priorities right. Occasionally, though, we may have to radically reorder our lives to ensure we are giving him his rightful place. And, sometimes, this has to be done corporately.

It is important that church members never elevate the church above Christ. There are those people who are happy to forego responsibility, who actually don't really want to grow up. It's so much easier to be told what to do. One time a young man came to me for counselling. From his look of concern I expected him to share a deep problem or some great difficulty. Instead his question was apparently quite trivial: he wanted to know if he could start dating a young woman in the church. I hesitated to give this kind of direction but rather spent time showing him how he could develop his own relationship with the Lord and become responsible for his own choices.

For some, a relationship with Christ that includes personally communicating with him takes too much involvement. They would rather a church leader told them what to do. Such folk are out of touch with Christ and content to remain that way. A church full of people who are out of touch with Christ is a church out of touch with Christ.

What or who controls your life?

The Lord requires of us a humble and teachable spirit – Scripture undoubtedly exorts us to submit ourselves one to another – but the fundamental control of our lives is a matter between ourselves and God. Anyone who abdicates this responsibility is, in effect, making a god out of something or someone else, in other words, committing idolatry. And it's possible for the idol to be the church or the church leaders.

It has to be said that the opposite is equally true: it is absolutely vital that church leaders do not begin to serve the church at the expense of their own personal relationship with Christ. This, too, is a form of idolatry. We can only serve the church as we hear how to do it from the head man! It is he who serves through us. When the priorities begin to slip, so does our relationship with the Lord. We are on the slippery slope to powerlessness and futility.

There was a time when we had to relearn some of these lessons at Kensington Temple. The church was growing in numbers and we had begun to backtrack from our early prayer emphasis. The pastors found themselves very, very busy. In the Wednesday prayer meetings we were preoccupied with counselling. The Bible study, which followed the prayer meeting, became the most important focus of the night. People would arrive intermittently throughout the prayer meeting, anxious to be on time for the Bible study and those people arriving early for counselling would pounce on the pastors if they caught sight of them in the meeting! As you can appreciate, there was a less than settled atmosphere. The interruptions were just a symptom of how much our prayer life was sliding away; we were losing focus, direction, fervency and power.

The leadership of the meeting was delegated to an elder. He had a good, strong ministry in prayer, there's no doubt about that, but whether he was annointed by the Lord to lead that meeting was another matter. It was an appointment of convenience. There was somebody else who could do it and we were grateful. Numbers began to dwindle. The vitality left. Effectiveness dropped. The leaders opted out. We were too busy.

When God speaks we'd better listen

God always speaks. So often we hear the words and we think, 'How nice of God to speak to us,' or, 'Oh, we must be all right because God is speaking to us,' and we altogether miss the point. Words have content. So do pictures. God is actually trying to communicate with us. There's something important that he wants us to hear. And not just to hear, but to act upon. So many words from the Lord are never acted upon and are eventually forgotten. Then we start to moan that nothing much is happening for us and where is God and why doesn't he do something about it? If this is you now, then go back to the things he has said to you. Look at them. Do you need to act on them?

In a place like Kensington Temple where there are such a large number of receptive Christians there might be a thousand visions before breakfast! It is sometimes easy to disregard the word of God because of the abundance of it. But this is dangerous. If God is speaking to us and we are living in him the Spirit will witness his truth in our hearts.

In this instance God called us through a prophetic word. There was a woman in the church who was given in her mind a picture of a vine. The roots were dry and the extremities of the branches were getting withered. I overheard someone talking about this and I had a strong witness within me that God was speaking. We discussed it at the leaders' meeting and acknowledged it was us, our church. Our roots were dry and we were overextending beyond what we were able to sustain spiritually and organisationally as well. We had to repent.

The first thing we did was to bring the leadership of the prayer meeting back into the senior leadership of the church. We started early in the day with various staff meetings and called for people to put forward how they felt God was saying we should pray that day. I would come prepared for this and we would pray together in the staff meetings.

Then I would spend the whole afternoon waiting on the Lord over those same prayer items, sometimes calling people in to shed more light on the workings of their departments and any difficulties they might be experiencing in them.

From the very first time we did this our church prayer meeting came alive as never before. The focus was on 'taking the city' and we drew our inspiration from the battle of Jericho found in Joshua chapter 6. There was an immediate sense of pulling together and as the whole church took up the challenge to prayer focusing on the real issues God had given to us. We felt engaged in a heavenly battle and had a real sense of moving forward in God's plans for us in the city.

We allowed the Spirit to lead us in everything. We stopped systematically trying to cover every aspect of church life in the prayer meeting; praying every item through and out was like wringing it dry of inspiration. Instead, we used the meeting as a spearhead. Just as soon as we began to break through in prayer we would move on to the next topic. We would then push the prayer emphasis out into our smaller groups and our own individual devotional times. People began coming to get the agenda for prayer, to get the inspiration and the anointing to pray for particular things. The following week would come and we would set the agenda again for another week so it became a week-long prayer meeting. Our prayers became specific, personal, powerful. The numbers doubled and doubled and doubled again until the spearhead became the most dynamic meeting of the week.

Pleasing the bridegroom

As we have seen, prayer is relationship and communication is as vital in our relationship with God as it is in any other relationship we may have. Developing a close relationship takes time. We can't expect to know everything about a person all at once. We must spend time in the Scriptures where we shall find the heartbeat of our Lord. Ask the Holy Spirit to unfold it to your heart. This is the place to learn wisdom and understanding; we can find out what pleases him and what he hates. We shall learn to tell right from wrong – something that we, all too often, take for granted. This is where we develop discernment: clear, spiritual sight. The great prayer concerns of God come into focus.

After he had prayed for the disciples, Jesus prayed earnestly for you and for me:

My prayer is not for them alone. I pray also for those who will believe in me through their message, that all of them may be one, Father, just as you are in me and I am in you. May they also believe in us so that the world may believe that you have sent me. I have given them the glory that you gave me, that they may be one as we are one. I in them and you in me. May they be brought to complete unity to let the world know that you sent me and have loved them even as you have loved me (James 17:20–3).

As we walk closer to our Lord we shall begin to tell the difference between spiritual mountains and fleshly molehills. We shall find ourselves together in spiritual reality, attuned to the things that are of overriding importance and holding loosely those things which are not.

Then we will no longer be infants, tossed back and forth by the waves, and blown here and there by every wind of teaching and by the cunning and craftiness of men in their deceitful scheming. Instead, speaking the truth in love, we will in all things grow up into him who is the Head, that is, Christ. From him the whole body, joined and held together by every supporting ligament, grows and builds itself up in love, as each part does its work (Ephesians 4:14–16).

You and I are being called to be part of that body. You and I are being called to be part of the true bride.

A true bride, blooming

Our God wants a true bride. He yearns for an intimate relationship with us. He wants us to walk with him, to listen to him, to learn from him. He has chosen us and will lead us and guide us. But we must be willing to follow him.

All over the world, those of us undertaking such a journey are united by the Holy Spirit who is living within each of us. Unity in the Spirit is a thing perceived and enacted in the Spirit of God rather than in pieces of paper bargained over by men. There are men and women who are today united in Christ even though their respective denominations would never agree on the small print. But such men and women, because they know their God, know also their brothers and sisters in Christ.

The body of Christ on the earth will continue to be built up 'until we all reach unity in the faith and in the knowledge of the Son of God and become mature, attaining to the whole measure of the fulness of Christ' (Ephesians 4:13).

Now that is an attainment worth having! And this is not some impossible dream – it is actually something that Christ himself intends to accomplish in us, by his Spirit. But we have to let him and we have to let him do it his way. Let's determine right now to examine our hearts and deal with them. If they are made of stone, seek him. He can replace stone hearts with hearts of flesh. Let's determine to allow him to mould us as he wills, then it can truly be said of us, 'his bride has made herself ready. Fine linen, bright and clean, was given her to wear' (Revelation 19:7–8). (Fine linen stands for the righteous acts of the saints.)

If we don't respond to his call the prognosis isn't very good. The further we drift from the vine, the more withered we shall become, majoring in minors, grimly clinging on to the small change of an impoverished faith. We shall become nit-picking, spiritually dry, self-righteous, mean and excluding, unattractive and defensive people: 'by their fruits shall you know them.' It will be clear to everyone except ourselves, of course, that we belong to the Lord in nothing but name. And what will the Lord think of us? We have the answer in the parable of the ten virgins (Matthew 25:1–13).

You remember the story – when the bridegroom

arrived only five virgins had oil to keep their lamps
burning. Only five were ready to go with him to the
wedding banquet. Later, the others arrived. ' "Sir! Sir!"
they said. "Open the door for us!" But he replied, "I
tell you the truth, I don't know you" ' (Matthew
25:11–12).

Jesus' earnest desire, even more, his command to us
is that we 'love each other as I have loved you' (John
15:12). Are we going to listen? Are we going to do it?
If the answer is 'no' then we shall be grieving the Spirit
of Christ within us and can expect to stay in the
wilderness where the Lord may sustain us but never
bring us out until we repent of our ways.

If the answer is 'yes', we are going to follow the
Lord's leading and walk in the love and truth of his
Spirit, then we shall be in him and he in us, just as he
prayed. No buts about it. And if you're abiding in the
vine you will bear fruit in season – it's a natural spiritual
progression. Out of this relationship springs every good
gift of God, including powerful, fervent and effective
prayer. 'You did not choose me, but I chose you and
appointed you to go and bear fruit – fruit that will last.
Then the Father will give you whatever you ask in my
name. This is my command: Love each other' (John
15:16–17).

5 Living in the Vine

Why not ask?

There really isn't a great deal of difference between developing our prayer lives and developing our relationship with the Lord. One can't exist without the other. We can never reduce God to rules and regulations but there are some basic principles involved in the relationship. Not being aware of the basics has caused many of us difficulties, if not extended spells in the wilderness. We can all do without that so let's take a look at some basic issues now.

Let's begin with asking. Asking is known as supplicatory prayer or a prayer of petition. Sometimes we (especially in the West) can have a strange attitude to asking, almost as if it's a bit indecent or unspiritual. Some of us have been brought up to view dependence on others as weak or sponging. Certainly, we don't want to be people who exploit others or who take all the time and give nothing in return. But this 'independent spirit' can cause trouble in all our relationships especially our relationship with God. In spiritual matters it is actually independence which is the unspiritual thing and dependence on God that is power and strength.

There is a sort of fatalism that sometimes stops people asking for things. This is the idea that runs, God knows what I need anyway so I don't have to ask him for anything. While it is undoubtedly true that the Lord knows our needs before we ask, the spiritual reality is that we are part of the equation, part of a relationship with him. He desires our communication. There is no place for the *que sera sera*, whatever will be will be, in his scheme of things.

Some people won't ask things of God because they feel it's inappropriate; they think that just presenting him with a shopping list is insulting. Well, if that's all they ever did, I might be tempted to agree but the fact is, and this is abundantly clear from Scripture, God *WANTS* us to ask!

'You do not have because you do not ask' God (John 4:2).

'Ask and you will receive and your joy will be complete' (John 16:24).

'And I will do whatever you ask in my name, so that the Son may bring glory to the Father. You may ask me for anything in my name and I will do it' (John 14:13–14).

'Ask . . . Seek . . . Knock . . .' (Matthew 7:7–11).

The Lord doesn't want us coveting, fighting and arguing for things. He states clearly that we shouldn't do this but instead we should ask him for what we need. He is not a begrudging figure who is far away from us. He is Emmanuel, God with us, our heavenly Father who delights in giving good things. He even gives good things to the wicked so how much more will he delight in blessing his children.

So often we take the human route and try to work everything out in our own minds instead of asking our heavenly Father. How many things have we missed out on simply because we failed to ask for them? Think, if we had brought to him all our secret visions and desires, where would we be now? Who would we be? What would we be?

Let it never be said of us that we missed out on his blessings just because we didn't ask! There may be times when we are led to ask repeatedly for something, sometimes over a period of weeks, months or even years. This calls for determination and persevering prayer which we'll come to later.

Timid praying

Don't mistake lack of confidence for reverence! We never have to creep to God; we never have to crawl; on no account are we to revert again to worm-consciousness. In Christ our sins are forgiven and the wrath of God no longer rests on us. That is what being saved means, it is what being redeemed means, it is the heart of Jesus' successful mission to rescue creation from its terrible inheritance of the knowledge of evil and the havoc that knowledge has wrought.

Jesus has lived amongst evil, has faced evil and has not succumbed. He was obedient to his Father even though it meant death and separation from him – something Jesus had never experienced before, something that for him was loathsome and deeply desolating. He stood in our place. He paid the penalty for our sins. He, though innocent, received the judgement that was due to us.

All those who receive Jesus, you and I, can walk free because of him. Our relationship with God is restored. Through the Holy Spirit within us we can walk in intimacy with God: Father, Son and Holy Spirit. When we come before our Lord's throne we can stand tall. Reverence and humility come from realising how much taller God stands!

Did you know that Jesus even commends us to be quite cheeky and break protocol with our heavenly

Father? Our God loves us much more than we appreciate. Trust him. Trust in his love. Our God isn't offended by boldness. Quite the opposite. He appreciates it and responds to it, even when our requests might, by universal standards, appear rather insignificant. If something matters enough to us, then it matters enough to our Father in heaven.

So much of what we need to know about prayer is contained in Jesus' own teaching on prayer (Luke 11:1–13). The man who wakes his neighbour at midnight to borrow some bread gets it because of his boldness: 'Yet because of this man's boldness he will get up and give him as much as he needs' (Luke 11:8).

The Greek word translated as boldness is 'shame-facedness' or 'cheek' or 'nerve'. We need the boldness and determination to think, 'I need X and I will not be put off by anything until I have obtained it.' We need to be unafraid of social protocols and conventions. Our Father in heaven doesn't sleep. If we want to get up in the night and beseech him to answer us he will be listening. Wherever we are, whatever the time of day or night, whatever our circumstances, our Father can hear us. What if we give him no rest? 'I have posted watchmen on your walls, O Jerusalem; they will never be silent day or night. You who call on the Lord, give yourselves no rest, and give him no rest till he establishes Jerusalem and makes her the praise of the earth' (Isaiah 62:6–7).

The whole of this very beautiful chapter of Isaiah describes the Lord's heart for his people, his yearning and intent to act. We, his Church, his bride, his partner, if we are in touch with his heart, then let us pray and pray and pray the concerns of our hearts. Let us give him no rest and we shall indeed see him establish his 'Holy People, the Redeemed of the Lord: and we shall be called "Sought After, the City No Longer Deserted."' (Isaiah 62:12).

May we approach the Lord with holy audacity! May we ask him for big things! He is big and we have direct access to him. We must not let the enemy limit us in how often we approach that throne or in what we ask when we get there.

'Let us then, approach the throne of grace with confidence, so that we may receive mercy and find grace to help us in our time of need' (Hebrews 4:16).

'Ask of me, and I will make the nations your inheritance, the ends of the earth your possession' (Psalms 2:8).

Do we know God's will?

'This is the confidence we have in approaching God; that if we ask anything according to his will, he hears us. And if we know that he hears us – whatever we ask – we know that we have what we asked of him' (1 John 5:14–15).

Prayer is a partnership. We are involved and should know God's will. This is how we receive the answers to our prayers. The important thing here is spiritual alignment, lining up with God's will. And this doesn't mean tagging 'if it be thy will, Lord' on the end of what we say.

An acquaintance of mine, Evie, had the following experience. Evie and her friend, Paula, were about to drive off to a prayer meeting. Evie hadn't long passed her driving test and she was nervous. It was dark, wet and windy and she hadn't been in the driving seat of a car for several weeks. She expressed her anxieties to Paula as they sat in the darkened car. Paula prayed, 'Oh Lord, please get us there safely, if it be thy will!' Quite apart from destroying any small confidence her friend may have been mustering, this reply tells us that

Paula was seeing God's will as something unfathomable, as unpredictable as a roulette wheel.

How can you be confident in someone unless you know they care about you, unless you know you can rely on their support? Things might not always work out the way we foresee or the way we intend; we can face hard and brutal circumstances in life but this ought never to shake our confidence in the Lord's heart of love and support towards us. Jesus tells us: 'In this world you will have trouble. But take heart! I have overcome the world' (John 16:33).

Knowing God's will comes from familiarity with God, familiarity with his ways, knowing him as a person. When we know someone intimately, we know their likes and dislikes, what they think about this, how they would react to that. This is why we need to walk intimately with our God. 'And I will do whatever you ask in my name, so that the Son may bring glory to the Father. You may ask me for anything in my name, and I will do it' (John 14:13–14).

Praying in the name of Jesus isn't a magic formula. It is a recognition that our authority and prayer is being exercised in alignment with the Father. It is to pray with the authority of Jesus, praying just as Jesus would pray because we know how he would pray.

Praying our own ideas

If we are not 'remaining in the vine' we are abiding somewhere else and the somewhere is usually our own selves. If we are not praying God's will in a situation we are praying our own and if we are knowingly praying contrary to God's will we are not even praying our own will but that of Satan. The following is all too often the subtext of our praying:

Our Father, who art in heaven,
Hallowed be thy name.
My Kingdom come, *my* will be done *in*
Heaven as it is *on earth*.

When we reside in our own ideas one person's 'Lord's will' is as good as another person's 'Lord's will'; just as good in different people's own eyes but just as erroneous in God's. There is one Lord and unless we are in touch with him we shall be going round and round in confused circles wondering why he doesn't answer us and discouraging ourselves and others in the process.

'When you ask, you do not receive, because you ask with wrong motives, that you may spend what you get on your pleasures' (James 4:3). Asking according to the will of God is asking according to the heart of God. Wrong motives can range from asking for more converts so that your church will be bigger than the one down the road and therefore you'll be considered more spiritual (the idols of self and church again) to pummelling heaven in order to get the latest status symbol.

There is nothing wrong with asking our God for blessings, for specific material and spiritual input into our lives. In fact, God wants us to ask, but how often we become self-obsessed. Where do our priorities lie? Are we making a god out of ourselves? Remember Jesus' words: 'But seek first his Kingdom and his righteousness and all these things will be given to you as well' (Mark 6:33).

There may be times when, despite asking the Lord and waiting on him, we are still not sure of his will in a particular situation. In these circumstances resist the temptation to make your best guess. The Holy Spirit himself knows the mind of God and can accomplish the necessary work.

In the same way the Spirit helps us in our weakness. We do not know what we ought to pray for, but the Spirit himself intercedes for us with groans that words cannot express. And he who searches our hearts knows the mind of the Spirit, because the Spirit intercedes for the saints in accordance with God's will (Romans 8:26–7).

The Holy Spirit intercedes for us according to the will of God. So when we are really not sure what the will of God is, the Spirit will pray his will through us.

Why do we doubt God?

There are two major issues about believing God: is he able and is he willing? Did Jesus ever turn anyone away? No. Never. People sometimes walked away from him because they could not give up what he required of them but he himself never counted anyone who came to him in humility too bad a case or too unworthy – even the leper who blew his cover in Galilee.

A man with leprosy came to him and begged him on his knees, 'If you are willing, you can make me clean.' Filled with compassion Jesus reached out his hand and touched the man, 'I am willing,' he said, 'Be clean!' Immediately the leprosy left him and he was cured (Mark 1:40–2).

Is God able? There is a sense in which this is a foolish question. How can the God who profoundly understands all the workings of his creation be unable to affect it?

We are back to the basics of spiritual reality! Our God has chosen to inhabit his Church. The question is not is *he* able? Rather it is are *we* willing? Why can't our God move through us as he desires to do? *We* have brought our God's reputation into disrepute: *we* have caused unbelief to flourish. Though it's no excuse, we're not the first to fail here.

Jesus came upon some of his disciples arguing with teachers of the law. A man had brought his son to them. The boy was in a dire state, possessed of a spirit which not only took away his speech and his hearing but caused him to have convulsions and tried to kill him by throwing him into fire or water. The man had asked the disciples to drive out the spirit. They had tried and failed. 'O unbelieving generation,' Jesus replied, 'how long shall I stay with you? How long shall I put up with you?' (Mark 9:19).

The father of the boy was losing faith. The disciples had not been able to help him. Now he wondered if even Jesus could. '"If you can do anything, take pity on us and help us." "'If you can?'" said Jesus, "Everything is possible for him who believes." Immediately the boy's father exclaimed, "I do believe; help me overcome my unbelief!"' (Mark 9:22–4).

Jesus cast out the spirit and the boy was healed. But the disciples couldn't understand why they hadn't been able to cast it out. 'He replied, "This kind can only come out by prayer"' (Mark 9:29).

So, the impediments here were unbelief and lack of prayer. For so long our churches have been filled to overflowing with unbelief and lack of prayer. Is it any wonder that we have been spiritually poverty-stricken? People have seen how impotent we are to change anything and have assumed it's because God is impotent too. This is why so many people have turned to mediums and psychic healers.

For many who have, as yet, little spiritual discernment, anything spiritual is better than nothing. How many people are aware of the warnings in Scripture about this?

> Let no one be found among you who sacrifices his son or daughter in the fire, who practises divination or sorcery, interprets omens, engages in witchcraft, or casts spells, or who is a medium or a spritist or who consults the dead. Anyone who does these things is detestable to the Lord.' (Deuteronomy 18:10–12)

We have failed to proclaim the full gospel and demonstrate God's power. So people have struggled with hurt and disappointment and have turned away in unbelief or blamed God for being unwilling to help them.

We have to undo this great harm. It is time to return to the source and inspiration of our faith, it is time to live in the vine, it is time to believe God, it is time to pray!

The prayer of faith

'Therefore, I tell you whatever you ask for in prayer, believe that you have received it, and it will be yours' (Mark 11:24).

'Faith comes from hearing the message, and the message is heard through the word of Christ' (Romans 10:17).

Faith comes by hearing from God. If you have heard from God over an issue, whether it be through a *rhema* word of scripture (that is when God takes a scripture and applies it directly and personally to your heart), through a word of prophecy or a word of advice that has witnessed in your heart, or something you have read or a direct word from the Lord – however God chooses to speak to you. If you have heard from him, you can be sure that he is already working to achieve the fulfilment of his word. When you have heard from him then you know you have what you have asked for.

As a church, we believe that God has spoken to us to take our city for Jesus. This will mean growing in effectiveness in every aspect of our corporate life and ministry until we can make a significant impact on the city as a whole. It will involve a very large network of fellowships and ministries reaching out from our central church and working together to achieve one goal: London for Christ. It is an awesome vision, even when we consider the partnership that exists between other churches in the city committed to the same goal. But our faith is rising to the challenge. With a confidence that comes from itense prayer we 'see' the results now by faith, even before they are achieved. It is as though the answer to our prayer is already in existence but not yet visible.

'Now faith is being sure of what we hope for and certain of what we do not see' (Hebrews 11:1).

Yonggi Cho, pastor of the world's largest Christian church in Seoul, Korea, calls this inner assurance of God's word being 'pregnant'. It's good way to describe it. It is as if you are incubating the answer to your prayer. It is already in your heart. The Holy Spirit within you bears witness that you have it. When this happens to us we can thank God because we know the answer to our prayer is already on the way.

This is asking in faith; this is the prayer of faith. When we ask for something in prayer we need to come to this position of faith. We must earnestly seek God and await his reply. Once we have it in our hearts our prayer is answered. Smith Wigglesworth said, 'If you have prayed five times you have prayed four in unbelief.' Once we have God's answer, to ask further is unnecessary, though we can always offer the Lord our joyful thanks!

There is, however, another mode of prayer – praying persistently. We may be asked to pray the prayer of persistence many times – the important thing is: however you pray, pray in faith!

I have to say in all honesty that we do have a gracious God who also answers prayers coming from weak, human hope, but the ideal is that we spend time waiting on him so that he can share his mind with us and turn our hope into faith. Then we are guaranteed our answer and the Holy Spirit can go about his creative work.

Praying for healing

My belief is that God desires to heal us. At the same time we must know that not everybody is healed. From the moment I met Robert, I could see death working against him. He was in the advanced stages of cancer and despite much prayer he died nine months later. He died trusting in Jesus Christ as Saviour and so his death was not a final victory for Satan. Robert died in the hope of the resurrection. But it is too easy to explain away the mystery of it all, to use the glorious prospect of our future with Christ in heaven as a cover up for the hard questions of today. This is often a pious mask worn by unbelief.

There is a tension between what we experience and God's willingness to heal which is so clear in Scripture: he never turned anybody away, never consulted a book to see whose name was on the list.

Sickness is not God's handiwork. He can use it as a tool but it doesn't originate with him. This belief doesn't come from trite persuasions and I say it with tremendous compassion for those not healed. When we pray for healing we don't simply quote Scripture at God, snap our fingers and say, 'There it is; we claim it.' We have to hear from the Lord. Sometimes we have to be sensitive to timing and understand how God may wish that healing to take place and sometimes we may need a diagnosis from the Spirit. Illness can have many roots, not all of them physical.

Also we have to be deeply conscious of the limitations of our whole environment. *We* are part of a 'blind and unbelieving generation', *we* are members of a 'perverse and wicked generation', as Jesus says in his teaching on faith.

In terms of the mainifestation of the fullness of Christ, the Church is still far behind. But seeing and acknowledging the problem is the beginning of turning round, of repenting, of allowing the Spirit of Christ to have his way.

God is a loving God, he is a generous God, he desires to place healing ministries among us, to make us a people of great faith – faith that will move mountains. Surely he desires to bless us and give us good things, therefore it is right to come boldly before him and ask for healing.

There are occasions when prayer is not answered in the way that we expect or the way that God encourages us to ask. Sometimes this may perplex us and we find there are mysteries that we have not yet understood.

When I pray for healing I never tag 'if it be your will' on the end of the prayer. I always think that's so lazy. If it's not God's will then why bother praying, and if I don't know if it's his will then I ought to find out and, if it is, have enough courage to pray it.

I was praying once for an elderly woman who was the mother of one of the pastors. She was well into her eighties and she was in a coma.

Well Lord, I thought, I can honestly say on this

occasion, I don't know whether it's your will to heal her or not. She's in a coma. I'm going to pray here, in front of this large congregation. Now in two or three days' time she's probably going to be dead.

I prayed for her healing but, just to ignore all my own advice, I did add 'if it be your will'. God is good, he is gracious and I'm glad he doesn't make us conform to hard and fast rules in our relationship with him. She was healed! She made a full recovery. The chances of her recovery from the coma were negligible but she returned as strong as an ox.

Sometimes our own minds can get in the way of what the Lord wants to do. We should never put our limits onto him.

Double-mindedness

But when he asks, he must believe and not doubt, because he who doubts is like a wave of the sea, blown and tossed by the wind. That man should not think he will receive anything from the Lord; he is a double-minded man, unstable in all he does. (James 1:6–8.)

Double-mindedness will always keep us in bondage. It is like accelerating and applying the brake at the same time. When we are moving in faith, the car is in gear: we can accelerate, we are singing along. But when we are double-minded we can't decide whether to stop or start, whether to turn right or left, whether to make the journey or not.

I'm sure we've all known double-minded people; I've known some who, I'm sure, are in more than two minds! There is the person who goes around asking everyone's advice about a matter only to find that everyone has a different opinion and, since their behaviour is dependent upon what other people think, they really are stuck!

Then there is the person who can never make a decision. Sometimes this is because they don't particularly care about either of the alternatives; there is nothing to weight their decision one way or the other; like deciding between eating a cake or a sandwich. So, they end up with neither.

Sometimes it is because they are paralysed with anxiety that their decision will be offending to somebody else and they just can't face any conflict at all.

I knew a young man who couldn't make up his mind whether he was called into politics or the Christian ministry. He dabbled in both for a while until it became apparent he was going to get nowhere until he was really clear about the direction he should be taking. Opting finally for politics he began what promises to be a fine career. He now has frequent contact with the decision-makers of our society and is able to offer them advice from his Christian perspective.

Some people are double-minded because they so desperately want to do the 'right' thing that they do nothing for fear of making a mistake. They just don't trust themselves. Do you know, the person who never made a mistake never made anything? Double-mindedness is rootless behaviour. It springs from fear and insecurity and it is a con. If you are double-minded, though you may not admit it, underneath you feel it to be the safest position to adopt, the position that will most save you from hurt and harm. But it is far from safe and far from pleasant. It is guaranteed to prevent you from achieving anything.

You might try to reconcile yourself to living such a shallow life that nothing matters very much; if life decisions can be reduced to the importance of cakes and sandwiches then it's no big deal if you miss out on them. Or you might spend your time following whichever wind blows next, settling for the shallow and short-term approval of others.

When we ask for something from God we are told we 'must believe and not doubt'. This doesn't mean that you are never allowed to doubt anything. We all grow in faith as we get to know God better. What it does mean is that you can't believe and not believe at the same time. You can't care and not care at the same time. You can't hold the two positions simultaneously.

Now do you see how much double-mindedness interferes with our prayers? There is no way you can pray with any kind of fervency if you can't bring yourself to really risk caring and, as we have seen, it is earnest prayer that avails much with God.

The cutting edge of double-mindedness is the ultimate doubt: has God changed his mind about me? Is he turning on me? When trials come upon us we need wisdom to understand where they're from and how we can meet them. James discusses this very problem and ends up like this: 'Don't be deceived, my dear brothers. Every good and perfect gift is from above, coming down from the Father of the heavenly lights, who does not change like shifting shadows' (James 1:16–17).

Determine never to allow the thought that you are rejected by God. That is a lie, a deception. God doesn't change. We can have absolute confidence in his goodness. Be single-minded: trust his perfect love. If you have no courage of your own you can lay hold of his courage. His desire is to give us wisdom, to enable us to care with his heart. He wants to turn the stranded and beached of this world into movers and shakers in his kingdom. Isn't that just like our God?

Forsake double-mindedness! Don't stay stranded!

Jump into the deep ocean of God's love and watch him bear you up.

Never give up!

The specific prayer of faith is quick, pertinent and effective. It rises out of God's own faith within us; we know it's what he wants to achieve and, when we pray, the answer is often tangible and immediate.

Sometimes we have to wait longer. We may have heard from God, we may know what he wants to do. Sometimes we can pray and feel that he has answered us; it is a 'breakthrough point', a sense of relief and confidence in the Spirit. But we may not tangibly see the result of our prayer for weeks.

Sometimes we have to wait even longer for answers. And there are times when the whole process is much drawn out. We may find ourselves travailing in prayer, beseeching God, sometimes with tears and fasting, and yet, though we witness his leading in our hearts, we do not reach a 'breakthrough point' and there is no sign of the answer we so desperately seek. This is the mode of prayer I want us to look at next.

What is needed here is the prayer of persistence. This mode of prayer is taught by Jesus in the parable of the persistent widow. 'Then Jesus told his disciples a parable to show them that they should always pray and not give up' (Luke 18:1–8).

This story revolves around a judge and a widow. The judge is a Godless fellow, unfeeling and indifferent to others. But, despite his grave shortcomings, he is someone in authority, the person who has the power to dispense justice.

The widow has been gravely wronged by an adversary. She keeps coming to the judge and pleading for justice. The judge turns a deaf ear. Her life is irrelevant to him. He can't be bothered with her. She's an irritation. She gets in the way.

But the widow doesn't give up. He is the man in charge; he is the man with the power to act; she has targetted him and she will not let the matter drop. It is important to her. She sets her face to be heard whatever the cost. She could have thought, 'Oh, if I bother him he'll clap me behind bars,' or 'He'll have me for disturbing the peace and causing a nuisance.' But no. This widow is going to be heard!

What happens? Well, the judge refuses to grant the widow justice and he persists in this for some time. Let's look at the widow's response. She could have quite understandably said, 'That's it now. I've given it my best shot and he didn't listen. I've no choice but to give up.' She could have gone home in despair and lived under a cloud of anger, rejection and depression.

What did she, in fact, do? She carried on. On and on and on and on. You can imagine that poor judge can't you? He gets up in the morning and there she is shouting outside his window. He goes out and she is there. He comes home and she is there. He goes to bed and she's in the street, shouting for justice. His head pounds; he's got a recurring migraine. At last he can bear it no longer.

Finally he said to himself, 'Even though I don't fear God or care about men, yet because this widow keeps bothering me, I will see that she gets justice, so that she won't eventually wear me out with her coming!'

And the Lord said, 'Listen to what the unjust judge says. And will not God bring about justice for his chosen ones, who cry out to him day and night? Will he keep putting them off? I tell you he will see that they get justice, and quickly. However, when the Son of Man comes, will he find faith on the earth? (Luke 18:4–8).

Our God loves us and he loves justice. If this man who cares nothing reponds, then how much more so will our heavenly Father who sacrificed his only Son to give us life. Jesus is telling us that we must never lose heart but, like the widow, we must pray and pray and pray, sometimes as long as it takes.

Giving up easily

Why do we give up too easily? How many problems would have been addressed, how many lives changed if only we had bombarded heaven with our prayers – and continued to bombard heaven.

In the West we are used to an 'instant' life. Instant light and heat; instant coffee; fast food; faster travel; stories at a glance (television/tabloids/comics). Deferred pleasure is not something we're particularly fond of. Yet learning how to defer pleasure, learning how to wait for results/answers/pay-offs is part of growing up, of maturing as an adult.

I think it is sad but true that many of us resist growing up. All too often we give way to that grabbing 'I want it now!' toddler within us when the Holy Spirit is trying to teach us peace, patience and self-control.

In the spiritual realm there are many things that are not, and in this age, never will be instant. (We shall examine some of them in closer detail later.) There are battles to be fought and victories to be won, relationships to be developed and processes of growth to be undergone. It all takes time.

Our God is the master of time and all that occurs

within it. Only he knows the end from the beginning. It is he who sets the seasons of our lives. And we must ultimately trust his wisdom.

Having said that, no one wants a great, long arctic winter; eleven months and three weeks of sub-zero temperatures, and one week of sunshine. That would be truly harsh even for the arctic and we shouldn't settle for it either. We should pray for all the good things we need. But when the answers to our prayers are delayed, we need to persevere, not give up. Perhaps we throw in the towel and settle for the arctic winter because we think it's all we deserve.

A pastor friend of mine who has a very successful teaching ministry was burdened for many years by a particular family pressure. A series of hurtful events in the church had left his wife depressed and physically ill. He found it almost impossible to carry on his ministry while caring for his wife in that condition. Nevertheless he hung on to God in prayer, quietly persisting day after day until things began to change. Dimly at first, the light appeared at the end of the deep tunnel that had closed around the entire family. After a while the pastor's wife began to recover and finally came right out of her former condition. She found her place again in the church family and her own. Friendship, understanding and counselling all played their part, but it was determined and sustained prayer that made all the difference. That's what living in the vine is all about.

6 Intercession: When, Where, Why?

The right ball game

Deciding how to pray is a bit like choosing a ball game. There are many, many ball games, each with its own set of rules. There are a variety of hitting instruments, from feet and hands to racquets, bats, cues and mallets. And the balls come in all sorts of sizes, shapes and weights, from table-tennis balls to rugby balls.

What would be your chances of potting a snooker ball with a croquet mallet or converting a try with a snooker cue? The wrong equipment and a resounding defeat is pretty much guaranteed. The right equipment but the wrong rules also spell defeat; you will be disqualified or give away penalties to the opposition.

The same is true of prayer. You won't get very far trying to intercede with a simple prayer of petition. We need to know how to enter spiritual conflict if we're going to win spiritual battles. Can you imagine a soldier going into battle alone and totally unprepared – no training, no discipline? What, do you think, would be his chances of survival? There have been too many casualties; too many maimed and hurting Christians are laid up in shock. It's time to draw a halt to the carnage. We have to come before our God and seriously learn what we're about. You can't play at

Christianity; the stakes are deadly serious: it's life or death.

As we have said, prayer is relationship, an understanding, something a million miles from a contract of rules and regulations. But there are principles that we can learn. These are not strict formulae like the rules of a sport but they are vital principles which operate in our relationship with God. To be unaware of them leaves us unfocused; answers to our prayers can turn too easily into hit-and-miss affairs which end up discouraging us. And sometimes the 'misses' and the penalties to the opposition rob us of the faith that has grown with the 'hits'.

This sort of apparently arbitrary exchange with our God can leave us feeling perplexed and vulnerable, our faith getting shakier and shakier. It has to be said that even when we seek wisdom and understanding we may not always be able to fathom out every situation we meet; we are only aware of the variables that God allows us to see. But he allows a lot for those who seek him. And he is certainly not arbitrary or whimsical.

If you are centred on Jesus, the rock, your house will stand whatever comes against it. You may find yourself unscathed or you may be left with a lot of bailing out and rebuilding to do; it's a bit like the difference between victory and survival. You were made for victory but the wind and rain may have lashed you hard, beaten you back and really shaken your confidence. Perhaps you have stood at great cost, but you don't have to be defeated. God himself is upholding you. Now is the time to learn from him about aggressive and victorious combat! Some of us have spent too long hiding in holes hoping for the dust to blow over.

In these desert storms we either cling to Jesus, our

rock, heed his words and persevere, or we start to doubt God's love for us; we wonder if he really is good and if his intentions towards us really are benign. Double-mindedness can infiltrate and tear us in two; we are almost afraid to look our God in the eye just in case we find our suspicions are correct. In our distress we turn away looking anywhere for comfort, anywhere for an answer, and, like the house built on shifting sand, we are ripe for a great fall.

This state of affairs is dangerous: unsatisfactory at best and lethal at worst. We find ourselves floundering when what we really need to do is to turn our attention to understanding and acting on spiritual realities. We need to know the appropriate type of communication for a particular moment. We need to know the right key that fits the lock to unlock a particular situation for ourselves and also for those the Lord lays on our hearts. When those storms begin to lash we have to know how to respond.

It isn't a matter of referring to the game rules. We need to come to God, wait before him if necessary, and ask him how he wants us to pray – which mode of prayer he would have us use. Prayer is, after all, his activity. Relying on God for direction as to how to pray just underlines the fact that we can't even begin without him; it is the Holy Spirit's leading which is the difference between praying our own ideas in a vacuum and bringing into being his creative will.

A prayerful progression

When we're speaking with someone we know well we don't usually analyse what we're doing. We don't normally think as we eat our breakfast, 'Oh, here comes my wife/husband/best friend. I'd better say hello, I'm going to, here I go, "Hello." Now what shall I say? Will she/he think I'm too intrusive if I ask her/him to pass the toast? Would it be too presumptuous to ask her/him to get me another cup of coffee?'

In discussing the finer details of how we pray there is a danger that we will become too self-conscious about talking to the Lord. The aim of this book is certainly not to get anyone so tied up in knots about praying the 'right way' that they stop praying altogether. Rather, it is to examine our relationship with the Lord in such a way as to facilitate prayer; to sweep away some of the obstacles and to shed light on barriers to the flow of his Spirit. Once we are aware of what's involved in this relationship we shall find ourselves more 'naturally supernatural', freer to flow between different modes of prayer, conforming to God's principles in the same way that we have learned to conform, almost without thinking, to the principles that underlie conversations with those we love.

There are many instances when different kinds of prayers overlap, when one sort leads inevitably into another, like different stages in a conversation. We have already considered prayers of petition or 'asking' prayers in some detail. Now it's time to turn our attention to a more profound mode of asking: intercession.

'I urge, then, first of all, that requests, prayers, intercession and thanksgiving be made for everyone' (1 Timothy 2:1) This verse mentions four types of prayer, all of which are involved in the process of intercession.

The first kind of prayer, 'requests', is described by the Greek word *deesis* which we have already mentioned. This means, you will remember, 'to ask out of a sense of need'. Here the need is uppermost in our hearts and we come before God with a sense of urgency. In intercession the Holy Spirit allows us to identify with others and feel their need; our prayers come out of that identification.

The second word in this verse, 'prayers' is the Greek word *proseuche* which, as we have seen before, means 'to ask in dependence on God for his provision'. So, having felt the urgency of the need, we are now coming in dependence on God, focusing on his ability to meet that need.

Next we come to intercession itself – in Greek *enteuxis*. This is a technical term for approaching a king with a petition. It also carries with it the idea of representing someone, of praying on someone's behalf. We shall examine this in more detail in a moment.

Finally we come to thanksgiving – in the Greek *eucharistia* which means 'offering thanks for the answers to requests'. Let's look again at the progression of prayer that can be drawn from this verse.

You begin by sensing a need. The Holy Spirit then shows you God's ability to meet that need. You intercede and pray on behalf of the person, beseeching the Lord to meet the need. Finally, you enter a time of thanksgiving as you feel a release in your spirit – the peace and assurance that the need has been met.

Who are these prayers of intercession intended for? 1 Timothy 2:1 says 'everyone'. We need to intercede for people who are searching for meaning in their lives, we need to intercede for the Lord's own people, the Church. Scripture urges us to intercede on behalf of those who govern us (irrespective of their political party!). We need to allow the Holy Spirit to lay on our hearts his concerns.

Churches in Europe are increasingly taking up their responsibility to pray for their government and those in authority over them. Recently in Britain the House of Lords Medical Ethics Committee met for a whole year to consider the question of euthanasia, or 'mercy killing'. The chairman had previously agreed to sponsor a bill which had been drafted by a society that was campaigning to see the introduction of voluntary euthanasia. The Christian position, which upholds the sanctity of life, was a minority position on the committee. The outcome seemed certain: a change in the law of Britain allowing for voluntary euthanasia.

In the event, the opposite was the case with a strong support for the hospice movement and a rejection of euthanasia. The decision was described as 'nothing short of a miracle' by Lyndon Bowring, chairman of the Christian action group CARE. There had been a mixture of gentle behind the scenes lobbying by informed Christians and much intercession. Most people were not even aware that the committee was sitting except the thousands of Christians who kept up a constant barrage of prayer. This victory was significantly achieved by prayer and can really only be sustained by on-going prayer.

There are no geographical boundaries to intercession. We can flow together with the spirit of God, touching whoever he wishes to touch, wherever that person may be on the planet. The overridding factor is to be in close communication with the Spirit of Christ within us and to be led by him.

The view from on high

When Jesus Christ ascended to heaven he sat down at the right hand of God the Father. All his earthly work had ended and he began his heavenly ministry. From this place of supreme power and authority, on the very throne of God, Jesus Christ ever lives to make intercession for us (Hebrews 7:25). This shows the Lord's attitude to prayer and intercession: his present ministry is totally dedicated to it. Jesus our heavenly intercessor is in touch with the Holy Spirit, the intercessor who has been sent into our hearts, and vice versa. That is how we remain in close contact and vital union with Christ; the Holy Spirit makes intercession for us according to the will of God and he is in unbroken communion with the Father and the Son.

That is how our prayers can be lifted above natural and physical boundaries and take on a truly supernatural dimension. The Holy Spirit can bring you right into the spiritual realm over a nation, over a situation, so that you can see it spiritually as clearly as if you are there physically. So much of our Christian lives and our ministry in the Spirit depends on our ability to see things from God's perspective. Unless we can see from God's vantage point we are going to be praying our own tired prayers, getting on our knees to worry rather than to make war on the enemy.

Intercession takes place in the heavenlies. What are these, you may ask? Scripture speaks of various aspects of the heavens. There are the heavens, meaning the atmosphere, the physical part of the universe. We see the heavens when we look out and count the stars.

We are told there is a realm of satanic rulership and domination. The 'ruler of the kingdom of the air, the spirit who is now at work in those who are disobedient' (Ephesians 2:2) holds sway on the earth. 'For our struggle is not against flesh and blood, but against the rulers, against the authorities, against the powers of this dark world and against the spiritual forces of evil in the heavenly realms' (Ephesians 6:12).

But there is yet another heavenly realm. There, in the highest place, God is seated in glory. Jesus has entered this place as our great High Priest. And that's where he is now: 'Christ Jesus, who died – more than that, who was raised to life – is at the right hand of God and is also interceding for us' (Romans 8:34).

Our Lord Jesus had thirty years of preparation, three years of public ministry, preaching and teaching and up to now almost two thousand years of intercession. Doesn't that show the place of intercession in the heart of God!

> 'Therefore, since we have a great high priest who has gone through the heavens, Jesus, the Son of God, let us hold firmly to the faith that we profess. For we do not have a high priest who is unable to sympathise with our weaknesses, but we have one who has been tempted in every way, just as we are – yet was without sin. Let us then approach the throne of grace with confidence, so that we may receive mercy and find grace to help us in our time of need. (Hebrews 4:14–16.)

Jesus is well acquainted with all aspects of the heavenly realms. He has passed through them and is seated with his Father. But what about us? Where are we? Read on!

Access to the throne

'And God raised us up with Christ and seated us with him in the heavenly realms' (Ephesians 2:6).

An earth-bound people cannot make intercession. We must grasp what it is to enter into the heavenly realms by faith in Jesus Christ. When God, by his Spirit, calls us to intercede, to stand in the gap for something of vital importance, we need to feel able to enter the heavenlies because that is where we belong. We need to understand that we have access to the throne room of God. And this is a very special kind of access – no debt, just credit. For life!

I find that the enemy has only two weapons: accusation and deception. When you begin to pray he can try to make you feel totally unworthy, accusing you and trying to deceive you into believing yourself to be a failure. (Let's face it, we do give him enough ammunition sometimes!) But, praise God, we can come to Jesus for cleansing; remember – the footbath?

So, what gives us access into the Father's presence? It is the blood of Jesus; the fact that he who was sinless has already paid the penalty for our sin by receiving the judgement due to us and dying in our place. Our righteousness doesn't take us through the heavenlies to the throne room of God, neither does our self-worth. Jesus' sacrifice on that cross is what has blazed our trail there.

When we come to pray, whether we are sitting in a bus or a church or a living room, we must realise that we are, in spiritual reality, seated with Christ at the right hand of God.

A people between

'Intercede' literally means in between. The principle of intercession is that you stand in between God and another person and represent them and plead their cause. Advocates or mediators are skilful people. They understand the culture and the temperament of those in question and they get alongside both parties. And this is how we, too, proceed. We know our God because of our intimate relationship with him. We have been given right of access to him, and we can come before him boldy because of the strength of our relationship.

The whole purpose of the coming of the Holy Spirit

into our lives is to bring us into intimate knowledge of God. He draws us closer and closer to Jesus Christ and God the Father. From this place of revelation we are able to communicate with God and share both our joys and our pains with him. This means we are also ideally placed to talk to God about the needs of others which we can know by straightforward communication and/or the Holy Spirit informing us supernaturally with a word of knowledge, or a word of wisdom or discernment. We'll look at the revelation gifts of the Spirit in detail later.

So, we are in the right place, with the *right information* and we have the authority to mediate or to 'intercede'. But this is no mechanical law court and we haven't had to slog ourselves into the ground for a law degree; this is the court of heaven and our qualification is our great ability and enabling in the Holy Spirit to represent others in the presence of God.

'But you are a chosen people, a royal priesthood, a holy nation, a people belonging to God' (1 Peter 2:9).

We have the authority to enter the presence of God through our great mediator, Jesus Christ, and we all have the authority to pray for each other. There is no hierarchy in this otherwise you'd have to submit your prayer requests to a certain class of people because they have access to God and you don't. The ministry of intercession is not a specialised function. Nowhere in Scripture is it mentioned as a spiritual gift apportioned to some and not others. Intercession is the role of every believer. When the Apostle Peter was in prison in Jerusalem they didn't call for the intercessors, they called for the Church. The Church prayed. And when the Church prays, something happens!

Will you stand in the gap?

Wherever God is at work he is looking for people to intervene and plead the case for others. He is looking for people who will have the heart of Jesus Christ, the great intercessor, people who will be prepared to come before him at the cost of their personal enjoyment and pleasure – and there is cost involved.

How would you respond to a modern-day Job? Remember the story? Circumstances were orchestrated by Satan in order to reduce this righteous man to total misery, to get him to curse God. His possessions were stolen and his servants murdered. His children were killed in an accident and then his whole body was afflicted with painful, pus-oozing sores. The book of Job is all about what he went through, his reactions and how he came to realise that he couldn't enter into the fullness of the understanding of God's purposes.

Eventually he comes before the Lord and the Lord restores everything to him; in fact, he ends up with twice as much as he had before, seven sons and three very beautiful daughters. But there is a point where Job cries out because he feels a great need for someone to represent his cause before God, someone who would be able to lay hold of God and himself and somehow bridge the gap; someone to mediate: 'If only there were someone to arbitrate between us, to lay his hand upon us both' (Job 9:33).

The Living Bible puts it like this: 'And I cannot defend myself, for you are no mere man as I am. If you were, then we could discuss it fairly, but there is no umpire between us, no middle man, no mediator to bring us together' (Job 9:32–3).

Job was in profound suffering and had an intense need for someone to stand in the gap. But what did his friends do? Did they stand with him and pray and encourage him? No. they accused him of sin and judged him. With friends like that who needs enemies? God was with Job and was angry with his 'friends', yet because Job himself interceded on their behalf, God forgave them and healed him. There never needs to be another Job suffering such great torment alone, feeling abandoned by God and people.

'Even now, my witness is in heaven; my advocate is on high. My intercessor is my friend as my eyes pour out tears to God; on behalf of a man he pleads with God as a man pleads for his friend' (Job 16:19–21). Job's prayer is answered in a prophetic way in the person of Jesus Christ. Jesus has become our advocate and pleads for us: he is the mediator between God and man through whom and in whose name we come before God. This role is also ours in Christ. The Lord is looking for intercessors to stand in the gap on behalf of others.

Crucial times

I looked for a man among them who would build up the wall and stand before me in the gap on behalf of the land so I would not have to destroy it, but I found none. So I will pour out my wrath on them and consume them with my fiery anger, bringing down on their heads all they have done, declares the Sovereign Lord' (Ezekiel 22:30–1).

There was a moment in the history of Judah, a point until which, if one person had been truly willing to stand in the gap before God on behalf of the land, the land would have been saved. There is a mystery here. I don't know why Ezekiel or Jeremiah could not have been that person. But the time came. And went. And it was too late. The principle is this: as we stand in that gap we can influence the destiny of our nation. Just one person in that critical moment would have been enough.

There are other passages in Daniel and Ezekiel that tell us just how bad the situation had become; that eventually, even if the greatest intercessor had stood in prayer, God would not have turned his wrath away, the people were so unrepentant. That may well have been the case but the point I am making is this: there comes a moment of opportunity when God is looking for us to stand in the gap, to build up the wall so that the Lord's greater purposes may be fulfilled. If we fail to respond then God is correspondingly influenced, not in his eternal purposes, but most definitely in how those purposes are outworked here on earth.

Then there are crises. In a crisis there are times when you can go so completely to pieces that emotional shock can prevent you from even praying. We really do need each other; someone else's prayers on your behalf can sometimes be vital, as can your prayers for another.

It might be as well to remind ourselves here that the throne room of God isn't filled with the deliberations of polite, but uninvolved bureaucrats. There is an aggression, a violence about the word 'intercession'. It is bursting through the double doors and presenting yourself before the King and saying, 'I have a petition.' There is a determination about it and when you're interceding there's an urgency. Never quench that urgency of spirit. The will of God and Satan are in conflict. Interceding often involves entering that conflict and prevailing.

Once, while we were ministering in Nigeria, the all-night prayer-group meeting here, in Britain, had a word from the Lord directing them to pray concerning

Nigerian children. They had no knowledge of exactly what was happening, but they felt they knew enough to start with – God often gives more revelation as you begin to pray.

This was the actual situation in Nigeria at the time: there was a plot to bribe children to start a riot where we were preaching. If that had happened who knows what the results for us would have been? But God alerted those people in Britain and they prayed until the threat lifted and not one stone was thrown. They were there, ready to stand in the gap. It is so necessary to have our spiritual ears open!

The prayers of the saints

How many of us, when we read a book, go to the last chapter to see what's happened? Well, God who knows the end from the beginning shows us in Revelation chapter 5 that we are in heaven. As we have already said, the great art of intercession is to see things from a heavenly perspective. So let's take a closer look.

Jesus is seated at the right hand of God. We are seated with him in heavenly places. In Revelation chapters 5 and 8, we see images of the prayers of the saints rising up like incense in the presence of God. This not only shows us that our prayers are effective in the throne room of God, but also helps us to catch a heavenly perspective of how God works out his purposes on the earth.

This is the inspiration behind special seasons of sustained prayer, such as a week of prayer, or a half-night of prayer. The church as a whole, or a group from within it, comes together to pray in an unhurried way free from the usual distractions. This is becoming a regular feature in many churches today, especially those that are growing and making an impact in their town or city. In preparation for a London-wide evangelistic campaign, intercessors from our church spent several successive nights of prayer. Throughout these special times of seeking God, it was as if our prayers were rising like incense to the throne of God. At the end of it all we were left with a deep sense that something had been settled by our praying. The mission that followed brought a lasting experience of God's presence and many came to believe in Christ, receiving God's forgiveness through him.

In Revelation chapter 5 we have a mighty angel who is at the right hand of the throne proclaiming in a loud voice, 'Who is worthy?' Then we have the elders, the seven eyes, the seven-fold Spirit of God sent out into all the earth, the four living creatures, the twenty-four elders and the Lamb. What else does God need?

In the midst of that heavenly scene we see the bowls full of the prayers of the saints. God is depending on you and me to pray. Can you imagine this scene if the bowls were only half full of incense? I venture to suggest that the book of Revelation would have finished there until they had been filled.

God was waiting for the bowls to be filled before the release could take place in which this revelation could be opened up to the Apostle John. Not only the revelation but its fulfilment – the release of actual events on earth depend as much upon the prayers of the saints as upon any other characteristic of Revelation chapter 5. So, when we talk about God's end-time purposes, we're talking about him calling up a body of believers across this world who will pray those bowls full of incense so that God's purposes may be released here on earth. It is a partnership as intense as that.

If you want to take your city or your country for

God, fill the bowl of prayer. When that bowl is full, God's purposes are brought to maturity and are released upon the earth, even as they are already released in heaven; his will is 'done on earth even as it is in heaven'. It is unthinkable that there will be a release of God's purposes on the earth without those bowls being full. So you want revival? Fill up the bowl. When the bowl is full, revival comes.

I'm going to tell you something surprising and exciting about what happens when you fill up one of those bowls. As I've found myself strategically placed by the Holy Spirit in intercessory prayer, I have at times harvested the fruits of intercession to a much greater degree than I have sown them. We tend to think 'this much prayer equals this much in results'. But it doesn't necessarily work that way. Of course, you're not the only one praying but when you are involved strategically in prayer and intercession, the rewards, the returns, are multiplied over and over. One of you will put to flight a thousand, two of you, ten thousand. We just don't know the power of believing prayer. But we're learning!

We are into very deep things when it comes to prayer and intercession but don't wait until you understand everything before you pray. God doesn't want people just to understand prayer – he wants people who pray! Even when our understanding is limited, if we pray and obey the Word of God then we shall see his mighty hand at work.

7   Intercession: How?

Hearing God's heartbeat

When you come into the presence of the Lord as an intercessor, very soon you will be in touch with the intercessory heart of Jesus Christ. It is impossible to come before God, whose heart is burdened with the needs of men and women, and not feel his heartbeat concerning some need or situation, even in majestic worship, praise or triumphant celebration.

This is what troubles me about some charismatic and Pentecostal praise and worship. We go into the presence of the Lord in a kind of party atmosphere and then say, 'Great! Thank you. Now it's time to go home.' If we stayed together in God's presence and waited on him for a while with hushed hearts, soon we would hear God's heartbeat and he would identify certain needs that he wants us to pray about at that specific moment. And then what mountains could be moved!

We need to wait, wait, wait on the Lord. We have to mean business. We have to understand the will of God before we can truly launch into intercession.

Did you hear about the man who made a new year's resolution to pray more? He wrote down all the things he thought he should be praying about. And he wrote. And he wrote. And he wrote. The list got so long that eventually he felt exasperated and so discouraged that he rolled it all up, put it in the waste bin and said, 'Oh Lord, thou knowest!'

If we spend our whole lives dedicated to it we couldn't possibly pray about everything that needs prayer. And we can't get round that by making our prayers really broad and all embracing. Then they just become so vague that they are meaningless. It's no good saying, 'God bless Africa.' Who do you want him to bless? And what does 'bless' mean here anyway? What do you want God to do? Where do you want him to do it? What does he want you to do? What does he want you to pray?

Of course there is the disciplined ongoing petitionary prayer that covers lots of areas. I have a basic principle that I follow when I pray. I pray for personal needs first of all because I think if I'm not getting blessed how can I pray for others to get blessed? God says, 'I will bless you and make you a blessing!' So that's how I begin – with my concerns. Then I move outwards. I pray for the church, then local needs, national needs and international needs. That is a regular, disciplined approach, but in all of it I'm constantly open to the Lord to lead me to identify with a particular need and to move me into intercession.

When coming to intercession never rush straight into prayer. Prayer is dynamic and not mechanical; Jesus tells us that we shall never be heard because of repetitious babbling: 'And when you pray, do not keep on babbling like pagans, for they think they will be heard because of their many words' (Matthew 6:7). The starting point of intercession is to empty oneself of preconditions and preconceptions and say, 'What is your will?'

What has God said?

The revelation of God's heart is the beginning of the move into intercessory prayer. We need to have a sense of God calling us to pray about an issue at a specific point. As we receive this revelation, an understanding of God's will in the situation unfolds, one step at a time. But we have to be open to this; it's a choice, a decision of will to move into it.

So many of us Christians in the West have had our minds educated rather than enlightened. Some of us have been stuffed full of facts and information at the expense of learning what it is to be involved with life, to identify with our world and the people in it. True revelation is when the heart is enlightened, when the 'inner person' perceives an unveiled truth. It is a spiritual process of communion between the Holy Spirit and humanity.

If you say to the Lord, 'I will identify with the leading and prompting of the Holy Spirit,' then you have to go where he wants you to go. You have given the Holy Spirit permission to use you when he needs to. It can be a dangerous prayer to pray, but it can also be a very creative one.

Once we have an understanding of God's perspective and his will in a situation then we are praying his agenda. That's marvellous! It's like a train running on railway tracks. I call it a 'prayer line' because it goes so smoothly. Of course there may be tough moments and the journey may be difficult, but you know you are making progress. You have a distinct impression that you are moving forward and achieving something. It's not random praying, not praying your will into existence but praying God's will, in God's way, in God's time. We see this happening over and over again in Scripture.

Daniel chapter 9 is a remarkable piece on prayer. Daniel is a captive in Babylon. One day, he's dong some Bible study on the book of Jeremiah when he realises that the Lord promised a seventy-year captivity for Judah. He looks at his calendar and realises that the seventy years are nearly up. It is almost time for God's word to be fulfilled.

I suspect that had most of us been in Daniel's shoes we would have rested on our laurels and said something like, 'Okay, that's great. God has said it; it will surely happen. We'll sit back and wait for it.' But Daniel didn't respond like that. Let's take a look at what he did.

Addressing the issues of captivity

When Daniel saw the will of God, even though it was uttered through an infallible prophet giving the very year that Judah would be freed from captivity, even though he knew all of that, the very first thing he did was to intercede. This was necessary in order that God's will could come to pass. That is how we should pray.

> So I turned to the Lord God and pleaded with him in prayer and petition, in fasting, and in sackcloth and ashes. I prayed to the Lord my God and confessed: 'O Lord, the great and awesome God, who keeps his covenant of love with all who love him and obey his commands, we have sinned and done wrong. We have been wicked and have rebelled; we have turned away from your commands and laws' (Daniel 9:3–5).

Daniel is a wonderful example of an intercessor. He received the revelation of God's will and also understood his role in bringing that will to pass on earth. He understood the nature of God and he understood the sinful nature of the people of Judah. Daniel sought God, coming before him 'in prayer and petition, in fasting, and in sackcloth and ashes' on behalf of the people. This man is serious. He is going back to the issues that led the people into captivity and he is asking for forgiveness.

Now I don't believe that anyone except the individual sinner is responsible for their individual sin. Nobody can stand in for anyone when it comes to individual responsibility. We cannot confess the sins of others, except through the principle of identification. When you really identify with a group of people you identify with that sin which needs to be brought before the Lord. Daniel confessed the sin of the nation because he realised he was a member of that nation and had the same roots in him, the fruits of which were seen around him.

God has poured out the measure of judgement he has determined. Daniel can now intercede for conditions of restoration: repentance and turning to God.

Recently the world watched as the nation of South Africa entered a new era. The relatively peaceful transference of power to black majority rule was heralded as a political miracle. The news media gave great attention to those in power and high-profile leaders were constantly brought to the international stage. However, what has not been so widely publicised is the groundswell of spiritual repentance and renewal that climaxed in earnest and intensive prayer. This took place in prayer meetings and churches of all denominations who turned their back on racism and cried out to the Lord for the deliverance of a nation. With more than 50 per cent of the nation professing Christian faith, this was surely the news behind the news and was perhaps the most significant contribution of all to the beginning of healing for South Africa.

Don't jump to conclusions

We have seen how the prophet Daniel knew that revelation was not, by itself, enough. Repentance and intercessory prayers were needed to bring that revelation of God's will into being.

Let's look at this same principle operating in the life of that mighty man of prayer, Elijah:

> Now Elijah the Tishbite, from Tishbe in Gilead, said to Ahab, 'As the Lord, the God of Israel, lives, whom I serve, there will be neither dew nor rain in the next few years except at my word' (1 Kings 17:1).
>
> After a long time, in the third year, the word of the Lord came to Elijah: 'Go and present yourself to Ahab, and I will send rain on the land' (1 Kings 18:1).

Elijah appears in Samaria, bold as you like, telling Ahab, the king, that it will only rain during the next few years on his command.

How can the pronouncement of anyone possibly affect the climatic conditions of a country? Our weather forecasters have enough trouble as it is and they've got all the benefits of satellite pictures and wind-speed measurements. Elijah's words could not evaporate the clouds or form them again or control the winds any more than yours or mine can. But God's word through Elijah could do all of those things.

Prophecy is God speaking. Elijah had received a word from the Lord that he was to speak in the name of the Lord. One great problem in the whole area of prayer, intercession, prophecy, spiritual gifts and ministries, healing and signs and wonders is that people say many things, supposedly on God's behalf, that God has not spoken. They are saying, 'Thus says the Lord,' 'This is what God is saying,' and God hasn't said anything of the sort. They are running ahead of him. Wait first of all for that revelation from God.

Praying a revelation into being

So, Elijah the prophet has heard from the Lord and he has spoken the Lord's heart. But this is not all that Elijah has done.

'Elijah was a man just like us. He prayed earnestly that it would not rain, and it did not rain on the land for three and a half years. Again he prayed, and the heavens gave rain, and the earth produced its crops.' (James 5:17–18).

Elijah soaked his pronouncements in prayer to the extent that he was able to say confidently, 'It's not going to rain until I say so.' Now that is a man who has sought the face of God and knows that what he's saying and doing is the will of God. He prayed the matter through; before the pronouncement or after it – or both!

After a long time, we are told, God said to Elijah, 'I will send rain' (1 Kings 18:1). The Lord determined when the rain would stop and when it would start again. How did Elijah respond? Did he sit around waiting for the divine nod? Whatever will be, will be? No he didn't. He understood his part in the spiritual realities of the situation. At the end of 1 Kings chapter 18 we find out what happened.

Elijah heard the sound of the rain prophetically; he knew that the clouds were on their way. Nobody else could see any sign of them but Elijah climbed to the top of Mount Carmel, bent down to the ground and put his face between his knees, deep in prayer. Seven times he sent his servant to look towards the sea and on the seventh time the servant saw a small cloud rising from the water. Elijah immediately knew that this was it! The answer to his prayer; the fulfilment of the Lord's will taking shape in physical reality. Before long the sky was black with clouds and a deluge of rain was falling on Israel.

We can receive the word of the Lord prophetically, pray that word, then (when we have the assurance and confidence) say, 'This is prayed through; this is now birthed; a reality; therefore I declare it.' This is praying a prayer of faith. But there are also times when prophecy comes out as will and intention. Once declared it must be prayed through into existence. Both ways of praying are sound spiritual principles.

The important thing is to know the mind of God on the situation. If we want to see effective answers to prayer then we must be praying what God wants us to pray.

Unless we are careful we can easily find ourselves way off mark. Our tendency is to put our interests and concerns above those of the Lord. Roland was determined to develop a video ministry. He had always had a love of technology and dreamed of using it for the gospel. The developing role of video in the life of the local church encouraged Roland to take some definite steps. Despite his wife Betty's uneasiness with the whole venture Roland sold his printing business and bought the expensive equipment necessary to start a small production company.

In all of this he did not wait for God's will to be clear to him. Rather, he assumed God was behind his efforts because it was all for the sake of the gospel wasn't it? A few months later his mistake became clear as Roland went through one financial crisis after another. No amount of praying could persuade God to bail out the project. There were no human agents willing to be persuaded either. Roland had stepped out of God's will for him.

If we're not praying God's will then we're praying against him. We won't see any answers that way!

Getting out of neutral gear

When we give our lives to the Lord we are doing just that. We shouldn't give him one day and not another. You either give something or you don't. You can't go snatching back your faith, your trust, your service – well, you can actually, but it's a one-way ticket to Sand City.

If we have given the Lord our lives we have not given him some intangible idea of the future. Our bodies belong to him; we become 'temples of the Holy Spirit'. Our minds are his to rule as well as our emotions, memories, intellects, and wills. And our own human spirit is his also. He lives in us, alongside us, reigning in the middle of our personalities, over everything that makes us human. This is submission to the Spirit of God.

When you come to intercede for a need, the human spirit engages with the Holy Spirit. The Holy Spirit knows that need through and through and when he is engaged in the process, identification with that need hits you. You feel it as if it was your own. That's what standing in the gap means – putting yourself in the other person's shoes. Don't try to put it on; the Holy Spirit doesn't want you working up interest or emotion.

This isn't a fleshly thing; it has nothing to do with acting, with worry or becoming submerged in someone else's character.

When we are in submission to the Holy Spirit during intercession, the identification with the situation being prayed for can be so deep that it is as if you were there. When we feel this identification then we know that the Spirit of God is at work. The gears are engaged. We can start to move.

I've got a little secret, a way that never fails in my own experience which I will share with you. I say, 'Lord, I come now and identify with this situation. I identify now with (whatever it is) and I want to pray for that, Lord. I want to stand in that gap in that situation.' I ask the Lord and as I am willing to come and stand in the gap I actually take up that position in the spiritual realm. It never fails. I find that as soon as I pray to the Lord like that he takes me at my word and I find myself, in spiritual terms, in the midst of that situation, actually identified with it.

When you pray at this level or even agree to 'be' that man or that woman, God shares his burden with you. At times I have almost expected my skin to turn black while praying for Africa! When I pray for Africa I *am* African. I become one of them. I am among them. If they've sinned, I feel it. If they're hurting, I'm hurting. I become a man 'from among them' who will build up the wall, who will stand in the gap.

The sweetness and authority of the throne room

Once a revelation of the Lord's will has been received and we are identifying with a revealed need we can begin to intercede. Reaching the point of intercession can happen in a moment or it can take months; there is no set pattern.

An intercession item is rarely resolved in five minutes and we must be prepared to be persistent. We should pray about the matter until we feel the release and God's burden lifting off coupled with a sense of joy and a flow of praise and thanksgiving. It is like giving birth, spiritually speaking. Often there is great agonising in the Spirit until the breakthrough comes.

Frequently when praying at these levels, there is resistance from the enemy. When you start to pray a real heaviness can come in and spiritual warfare is needed before the breakthrough comes. If this happens to you, be wise. There is no place in a war for the lone soldier wandering about doing his own thing. You must know what you are doing, that God wants you to be doing it and that you are alongside fellow-fighters under spiritual authority. That is the way to victory! Alone you are very likely to be picked off by the enemy. I am speaking from experience. Believe me – we need each other. Don't be put off. Be wise. And advance!

This level of praying is the most exciting part of ministry. In intercession I needn't leave my study yet I can influence the world. I can lift up other ministries in prayer and share in the fruits. But even more, there is such a sweetness about being with Jesus in this place of prayer.

To know that identification with the Holy Spirit, to be so close to God that you feel his heart beating next to you, I tell you – there's nothing like it! I wouldn't exchange it for anything. In fact I would exchange everything just for that! In that place there is such authority. I've been under greater anointing in intercession than in anything I've ever done in public. In intercession I've been able to speak the destiny of nations and I have seen it unfold in reality before my very eyes – this is not just something that happens in your imagination.

In 1986 I went to West Africa. It was my first trip back into Africa in ministry; 1987 arrived and with it the next African conference. I knew it was someone else's turn to preach but how I wanted to go again! It seemed impossible. Then God said to me, 'You *can* go. You pray as if you were going.'

So I got down on my knees and began to pray for that particular country. I said, 'Oh God, I enter into the gap right now on behalf of these people.' Immediately I found myself in a barren place, a wilderness. It wasn't exactly a physical vision, but real enough for me to describe it that way. I was seeing these things in my spirit. I saw a dry land and trees which were newly dry. Something had gone wrong and I cried out to God in this place. It was such agony. I said, 'Oh God, why is it so dry?' Suddenly I was a man among them, not just trying to work up some sort of prayer or discipline for another nation on another side of the world. I was *there*, in the realm of the Spirit.

I began to cry out to God. I can't describe what it felt like. It was awful. It was as if I had the heart of God for the nation. God had spoken to me. The dryness was desperate. I began to pray, to cry out, to seek the face of God over the situation. It was as if that nation had entered into slavery. Years ago slaves who had been freed had settled in the capital. God said to me something like this: 'In that time (I knew very little of this history!) I brought them back to be free in me and yet they have rejected me and refused to give me the glory. Therefore I have withheld from them.' It was like a spirit of captivity. I prayed and interceded about this.

About a year later an evangelist from the church in

London went and conducted the biggest crusade in the history of the nation. Not much more than five hundred people attended at any one time but two thousand responded to the gospel message in the space of four days! Since that time other international evangelists have visited with huge results. But in that one situation, God had put me into the realm of the Spirit over that nation.

God's burden

I'm going to share with you some more from my own intercessory ministry. There are certain features of it which might be peculiar to me and I don't want you to assume that if it's not exactly the same for you then you haven't got what it takes. This is absolutely untrue. We are all individuals at different stages of growth, doing very different things in the kingdom. Begin where you are. Don't overreach yourself. Bring intercession together with every other principle of prayer you already know about.

In 1988 I was in a city in another part of Africa. I hope you will forgive me for not naming these places; to identify them may well put people's lives at risk and curtail the work of God. Let's just say I was somewhere where you can feel and smell the Sahara desert! I was meeting with other Christians and we were focusing in prayer on what lay across the Sahara. We wanted to begin to bring the gospel to our Moslem friends.

A brother who desperately wanted to be with us travelled all through the night and the following day, broke a curfew in one city and drove all the way to our meeting place. Having found us, he wanted me to come and spend a couple of weeks in his church. I had so many commitments I had to refuse. He had faced danger and hardship to reach me and I couldn't even give him one day. I was troubled by it.

That afternoon I had to get washed, get my message prepared, pray, have a rest and eat, all in about an hour and a quarter. When you're on missions you understand it'll be like that. To do it all you have to do several things at once. And yet during this time God gave me a strategy of how to reach these people and showed me what to do about not being able to be everywhere at once. We could start Bible courses! From that moment, God's burden for that part of the world entered my spirit.

Reaping – the privileges of intercession

Several years later I was invited to go back and help lead a mission in that same African city. Whatever their national constitution says about freedom of worship, due to the influence of Islam things were very different in that place.

On the first night, our host preached a powerful message. Many people came to Christ but they were mainly people from the more open southern part of the country who only worked in the north. On the second day I excused myself from everything. I needed a whole day free to spend in prayer. I was to preach that night and I knew that either God was going to move or nothing was going to get done. So I prayed and marched up and down that hotel room, one hour, two hours, three hours – I can't remember how long – until I got so frustrated I said, 'Dear God, I'm only flesh and blood. I need your anointing. If I leave this hotel I may not even be back.'

We were having to take a different route each night to the mission ground, we were so unpopular with the extremists there. Then there was an incident which was either an attempt on my life or a bid to frighten me off. Somebody had tampered with the wiring in a light switch in my room. Had I been earthed or touching the switch with wet hands, I would have been killed. As it was, I got a nasty shock.

The local people said, 'Don't stay in this hotel, you are too vulnerable. We'll hide you somewhere.' But the Holy Spirit had already given me a word – 'they will not harm you', so I said, 'I'm standing on the promise of God, no problem.' Sounds brave doesn't it? I tell you if I hadn't had that word I'd've been first out of the door!

I paced up and down my room and said, 'Dear God, I'm just Colin Dye and I know I can't do this. Oh God, what am I going to do?'

Then I felt God say to me, 'I have brought you here to see the firstfruits of this harvest. Others have sown with their tears and with their blood but it is for you to begin to reap this harvest because you have been faithful in intercession.'

God gave me a great privilege. He also gave me a verse of Scripture which released faith and as I walked forward I 'stepped' from one realm into another, from a blind and deaf place into one where new laws were applying, where blind eyes could see and deaf ears could hear, in the name of Jesus. I was anointed with such faith!

I went to that mission ground and I preached a clear gospel message directly into the situation and hundreds of people started to come forward. This was in sight of the secret police, in a place where, if you convert from Islam, you're liable to severe persecution. You can lose your family, your job; you can even lose your life.

So many people came forward right in front of the police who were there to identify converts. How many others must have been standing in the crowd? I said to the people, 'If Jesus does not heal the sick, then he is not Lord.' I said, 'If Jesus does not touch people's lives tonight then he is not risen from the dead. Now we shall see who is Lord.' Then I called down the fire of God and people were healed. Many saw what happened and flocked to Christ. It was the breakthrough we'd talked about and since then that same ministry and others have gone into one city after another so that all heaven is breaking loose!

You cannot submit to the Spirit of intercession without cost. There are times when I have closed the door on my wife and my family or got up in the middle of the night when the Holy Spirit has prompted me. I've set aside days of prayer and fasting and entered into the presence of the Lord and pleaded and interceded over the nations for which he shed his blood. I have then stood at the place where God has given me the privilege of setting the whole thing alight, of bringing in the first fruits.

What will it be like on that day when, in heaven, he shows us those bowls of incense overflowing? He'll say, 'Thank you for your prayers. You released the blessing upon the nations of the earth.'

I think that's going to be more wonderful than anything I experienced in Africa. And there will be some surprises too. People at the front of that queue of commendation will be surprising people. People we never knew about. People we never met. There will be people standing in front of me to receive the reward from Jesus, people who prayed for me at that crusade. That's the ministry of intercession. That's the heart of God.

8 Praying Together

An ear to hear

If we are 'remaining in the Vine' as individuals then when we come together to pray we can be a powerful, formidable army, able to change things in the heavenly realms, influencing the world in which we live and bringing into being God's creative will. This is how things should be! Unfortunately it doesn't always happen. There are often specific impediments to the powerful, corporate prayer life of a church.

I have already described to you how, having gained vital insights into the importance of prayer, we as a church slid away from our initial prayer emphasis and as a result began to lose power and effectiveness. We had to come before the Lord and repent. We had to change our way of thinking and turn our priorities right round. To do this we needed to know we were moving in the will and way of God; we needed to be open to receive his focus and direction, not only individually but together as a church.

The most important starting point, individually or collectively, is a revelation from God. It may be helpful here to quash some erroneous ideas about receiving words from the Lord. It's amazing what some people will try! You cannot hear from God by shutting your eyes and sticking your finger in the Bible. I heard of someone who did that. The first effort produced, 'And Judas went out and hanged himself.' The second produced, 'Go and do thou likewise'!

Nor can we pick a promise from 'Granny's Promise Box'. This is a container with many Scripture promises printed on tiny cards or rolled-up pieces of paper. You are meant to pick out a promise at random, praying if you wish, as you do it. The strange thing though is how one sided these 'promises' are. They say nice things like, 'Take heart, I have overcome the world,' but conveniently forget the other part of the same verse that says, 'In the world you will have trouble' (John 16:33). This is reducing the Word of God to the level of a fortune cookie. We are not in the business of the trite, the sentimental or the superstitious. We want to hear from God.

If you want to know the sort of things the Lord would have you pray you must know Scripture, but not use your knowledge merely in an academic way. For example, don't say, 'We need to evangelise so let's turn to the end of Mark 16 and pray that.' That is human reasoning. We need to start by praying, 'Lord give me an understanding of your will in this situation.' Often the answer comes as a specific Scripture. Sometimes it will come by listening to a tape or a sermon or by a word of confirmed prophecy. Sometimes just standing in the bus queue a verse will spring to mind and you will know emphatically that the Scripture *is* the will of God for that situation.

There are two safeguards that you can use to ensure that you are not straying off track. The first is to remember that the Lord never asks you to do anything that is expressly contrary to his revealed will. That is why lack of scriptural knowledge can make you vulnerable. The other safeguard is the response of the Holy

Spirit within you. If your life is submitted to him his peace will act like an umpire; you will lose it when you are straying off course.

Once we have heard from God, his word then becomes a 'prayer line' – a track that you can get on. We can pray knowing that God is behind what we are doing, like a locomotive. The church prays with everyone moving in the same direction. Corporately you become like a very powerful battering ram.

A house of prayer

At about the same time that the Lord was speaking to us over the issue of our ailing corporate prayer life I had a vision, a picture in my mind's eye. It was a picture of a house with the pillars crumbling away. The Lord said, 'This is the house of prayer and I want you to repair it.' The pillars that were crumbling were the pillars of prayer.

The Holy Spirit brought to our attention a Scripture: 'My house will be called a house of prayer for all nations' (Mark 11:17). This Scripture then became our 'prayer line', the general thrust of what God was saying to us. Then we had to look at the specifics. We had to ask questions: what is stopping us; what is standing in the way of this church being a house of prayer; what specifically needs to be restored?

When we turned our attention to the problems we found apathy, slumber, civilian mentality (which I'll explain more about later), and the spirit of prayerlessness itself. We prayed against these things. In this way we re-established prayer in the life of the church.

When God speaks you have to listen and you have to implement what he says. When he speaks into our church like this we spend months, in this case six to nine of them, concentrating on this one thing alone.

Another very strong prayer line that God gave us as a church was from Isaiah: 'No longer will violence be heard in your land nor ruin or destruction within your borders, but you will call your walls Salvation and your gates Praise (Isaiah 60:18).

We prayed this single prayer line intensely for months, in fact we were continually coming back to it over a period of about five years. Obviously we didn't address it at every meeting in a tedious way, but we were continually seeking God about it, meditating on it and coming back to it again and again and again.

Praying this specific word from the Lord to us was a very, very powerful thing because it loosed so much of the life of the church. Our willingness to release praise to God was touched because our gates were to be called Praise. This was the entrance to everything and we prayed that we and everyone who entered the church or who was connected with us in any way would be touched by a real spirit of praise and thanksgiving. And that really did break forth.

Our walls were to be called Salvation which spoke to us of evangelism. The picture we had was of the church (both the building and the people) being a surrounding wall. People who entered the building or who came into contact with us would be saved because they would be in a prayer environment, a prepared environment.

At this time we were also thinking of Yonggi Cho's church in Korea. So many Christians are praying there that Cho is able to cite examples of people becoming Christians who, outside Korea, wouldn't have given Jesus a second thought. It's the positive side of spiritual warfare. We began to pray along these lines, to prepare ourselves and the church building itself. We even laid hands on the walls.

Prayer and preparation is not abstract; it's not all sweet stuff in the heavenlies – it's very real. When you are ready you have to be able to answer the question, 'Now who do I want here?' We knew who we wanted. We asked God specifically for occultists, drug addicts and gangsters. And they started to come in and turn their lives over to God! We even had Triad gang members coming from Hong Kong, attending meetings and becoming Christians.

Outside the house

About a year later the part of the prayer line concerning ruin and destruction became very significant to us. There were relationships in our church under threat of destruction and at the same time the IRA stepped up its terrorist bombing campaign in London.

We, along with many others, began to pray purposefully against violence, destruction and ruin with specific regard to the IRA. Extra vigilance paid off and spot checks revealed bombs 'quite by chance', preventing major catastrophies. There was a lot of disruption but the mass injury, death and destruction sought by the IRA didn't occur. After a lull there was a final enormous explosion which did a great deal of structural damage – we (and most likely others too) had stopped praying, believing the campaign to be at an end.

Another very strong example of the battle with destruction, ruin and violence in our area can be found in events surrounding the Notting Hill carnival. This is one of the largest carnivals of its kind in Europe and it lasts for several days. Since we started having all-night prayer meetings and strong prayer into this situation, the carnival has turned right round from an event that was becoming synonymous with drugs and violence, to a peaceful, colourful and happy event. It's getting more and more peaceful each year. That really coincides with times of strong, collective and combative prayer.

Praying in large groups

There are now so many in our church that in order to meet all together we have to hire the Royal Albert Hall or a large ten-thousand-seater arena. It's tremendous when we can do this but obviously it's not something you can do every week! We are split, for most of the time, into satellite churches that meet throughout London, although we do have regular large celebration meetings too. The feel and operation of larger meetings has, by definition, to be different to that of the smaller groups. The more intimate a prayer group is the more room it will be able to give to sharing and greater spontaneity in the use of gifts of the Spirit. It is easy for the group leader to oversee and, if necessary, keep the prayer purposeful and on target.

Prayer meetings need strong focus and direction. They also require a leadership who will be listening to God all the time and have a sense of what he wants to do next.

First we need to know the Holy Spirit's agenda for that particular meeting. Then we need a prayer line for that, something we can all get behind and pray through. And finally we must know which mode of prayer we are going to corporately use.

At KT we stress the role of the leaders, those who have a proven record and whom we can trust to be seeking and hearing God's direction for the meeting – that doesn't mean others won't also seek the Lord but there must be people who will take the responsibility for finding out what the Holy Spirit's agenda is for that meeting. These leaders need not only the integrity to spend time waiting on the Lord for his direction, but they must have developed spiritual ears sensitive to the Spirit's leading.

Sometimes the meeting will major on praise and thanksgiving, sometimes we might break up into smaller groups, especially for the gentler kinds of petitionary prayer. (That is, prayer in which we simply ask God for the answers to straightforward requests for ourselves or others.) At other times we may be in a loud warfare mode. It is up to the leaders to be adaptable – always open to what God wants to do. There have been times when I've come to lead a meeting with four or five things to pray through and haven't got past the first one!

In these larger meetings if someone from the congregation feels that God has given them something to contribute they do not have immediate access to the microphone. It is so easy for the prayer dynamic to be sidetracked. There are people who, given half a chance, will hog or hijack a meeting!

Nevertheless, God can and does give important contributions to people in the congregation. In these instances, people can approach the platform and discuss what they have to say quietly with someone there. When the contribution has been recognised as being relevant for that moment, the leader is informed at an appropriate time during the meeting.

I feel it's a mistake to try and pray solidly en masse for too long a period, although we are always aiming to extend the amount of time we spend praying. It's important to bear in mind that we are all human and in a large group people's ability to concentrate will vary greatly. We have to pace ourselves and not drive each other hard. Remember – the shepherd leads; the butcher drives!

Prayer at KT is interspersed with the input of different ministries, teaching or worship. It's like feeding the troops. You can't get a depressed or despondent people to pray victoriously. You have to be real and address people where they are as they are. I am willing to work hard for fifty minutes even if it only means ten minutes of effective corporate prayer at the end of it. You can't judge the quality of prayer by the amount of it. I'd rather have ten minutes of powerful, creative prayer than an hour and a half of wishy-washy ineffectiveness.

Nights of prayer

In most churches you can find people who are more motivated to intercede than others; those people who are responding to a very strong prayer calling. These are the people who are the core of all-night prayer meetings and, of course, the bigger the church, the larger this core of dedicated prayer warriors is likely to be.

When we meet for nights of prayer we know we can rely on this core of people. Sometimes there will be others who perhaps wouldn't normally come but who feel the importance of praying for the goal of that particular meeting. Again, the larger the congregation of a praying church, the bigger this meeting is going to be.

During the nights of prayer you always have to remember that people are going to get tired, they're going to need a rest here and there. We break the night up. Bouts of praying are interspersed with teaching, praise, worship, testimony, then, when you catch the wind of the Spirit, you just sail and flow from prayer to praise to intercession to thanksgiving, this area, that area, then warfare: the variety of it is what sustains people.

It always helps to vary people's posture. Depending on what the Holy Spirit wants to achieve, we might find ourselves kneeling before God and waiting on him in silence or we might clear away the chairs and find ourselves marching round the room.

The way in which we express ourselves in prayer should reflect the nature of what we are saying. You don't go to a football match, watch your team score a goal and quietly and politely say, 'Oh, that was nice wasn't it?' If we are being real people with God (and nowhere does he suggest that we become timid and religious the minute we approach him) the form and tone of our conversation will be determined by the things we are saying and the attitudes behind them. We can pray loudly; we can pray softly or even silently.

Perhaps we need to remind ourselves at this point that we are never heard by God because of our volume or lack of it. God looks on the condition of our hearts and our faith in Jesus. Let's look at two scriptures here:

During the days of Jesus' life on earth, he offered up prayers and petitions with loud cries and tears to the one who could save him from death, and he was heard because of his reverent submission (Hebrews 5:7).

The king said to me, 'What is it you want?' Then I prayed to the God of heaven and I answered the king (Nehemiah 2:4–5).

Here is an example of Jesus praying with loud cries and tears and another example of Nehemiah crying out to God in total silence for wisdom to answer the king.

When it comes to speaking with God, let's come as free men and women not as slaves of our various cultures. The important thing is the heart and its motivations. Are we, in Britain and the West, afraid to pray loudly because of our reserved culture or our own timidity? Perhaps we pray loudly all the time. Do we think God can't hear us? Or do we want to make sure other people do? When we pray together in large groups we must be prepared for times of silence and waiting on God. And we must be just as prepared for the flow of the Spirit as he does his work among us, sometimes taking us into great crescendos of prayer. Let's be appropriate. Let's be real with God and each other.

The principle of agreement

In intercession, as in prophecy and witnessing, groups of people or whole churches can function under a corporate anointing; power is multiplied and tremendous battles can be won. 'Five of you will chase a hundred, and a hundred of you will chase ten thousand' (Leviticus 26:8). There is a powerful principle at work here – the principle of agreement.

> I tell you the truth, whatever you bind on earth will be bound in heaven, and whatever you loose on earth will be loosed in heaven. Again, I tell you that if two of you on earth agree about anything you ask for, it will be done for you by my Father in heaven. For where two or three come together in my name, there am I with them. (Matthew 18:18–20.)

In this passage Jesus is drawing on the biblical principle that a thing is established by two or three witnesses (Deuteronomy 19:15). This is to ensure a certain amount of safety and direction. We can keep each other in check and ensure that goals are in clear focus.

This 'whatever you bind, whatever you agree on' passage is about coming to God in Jesus' name not our own name. It is about aligning ourselves corporately with God. It is not about trying to manipulate him. It's no good two people ganging up on their way to pray. You can imagine it, can't you? 'You agree with me for a husband and I'll agree with you for a Rolls Royce!' No. This won't cut any ice with God. These verses are not about finding a way of enforcing our will, agreeing together what we want and then making God comply (even if we think we've planned a wonderful tent campaign!). These verses are about knowing the will of God and agreeing together about what he wants.

The original literal translation from the Greek runs like this: 'I tell you the truth, whatever you bind on earth *shall have been bound* in heaven, and whatever you loose on earth *shall have been loosed* in heaven' (Matthew 18:18).

Our task is to discover the things that are already accomplished in heaven, those things that are planned in the purposes of God! If we pray according to God's plans then we are bringing about his creative will and in that way God's will is done on earth as it is already purposed or done in heaven.

There is a danger in misunderstanding these verses because this kind of corporate prayer is so powerful that you may find yourself tempted to think that you or your group have some special 'hold' on God. This is a great deception leading not to faith but to unreality. And this kind of pride comes before a fall. Avoid the trap. You can't fail, really, if you ask, 'Lord, what do *you* want to happen?'

So when we come to pray together we align ourselves with God and agree together about his purpose for our

meeting. We can expect to experience the power of
unity and corporate anointing: a moving together in the
Holy Spirit.

A ministry of help

'When Moses' hands grew tired, they took a stone and
put it under him and he sat on it. Aaron and Hur held
his hands up – one on one side, one on the other – so
that his hands remained steady till sunset' (Exodus 17:12).

Intercessors must always remember that their role is
a supportive one. I think that what Moses, Aaron and
Hur didn't do on this occasion is as telling as what they
did do. Aaron and Hur supported Moses. They didn't
say, 'You're obviously too exhausted for this, Moses.
Why don't you go and have a lie down. Put your feet
up. Don't worry, we'll take over while you're gone.'
That would have been usurping Moses' authority.

And what about Moses? There was a battle raging
and he was very tired. The victory depended on his
relationship with the Lord. He had the staff of God in
his hands. When he held it high the Israelites started to
win the battle but the moment he lowered his hands
they began to lose. He could have asked Aaron and
Hur to take over. He could have excused himself. He
could have said, 'My arms are so tired and I've got to
hold this up until sunset? I can't possibly cope with
that!' Instead of sticking to his appointed task, hard
though it was, and allowing others to support him, he
could have abdicated leadership. Happily, he didn't.
And the Israelites won the battle.

Personal prayer has to be the number one priority
for any church leadership. Leaders must be truly living
in the vine and would be extremely foolish to delegate
their prayer responsibility to others, even prayer lead-

ers. Where this happens they might keep the title of leader but the real leadership of the church will eventually reside elsewhere, often with disastrous results. I have seen it happen again and again. And it is easy to see how.

There are always people who are keen and available. They are quite often, though not always, women who are at home. That isn't an unfair remark, it's just what I know from experience actually tends to happen. These are the people with the time and they are all set to pray. There's nothing wrong with that. It's potentially a tremendously powerful thing. So far, so good.

The leader of the church is very busy, or feels, like Moses, exhausted. Too overworked, in fact, to pray. Now there are some willing and available people who are all ready to pray. It looks marvellous, the answer to everything. The leader, too busy to spearhead the prayer, delegates the job to someone else. This is where division comes from, time and time again. Let me unravel it a bit further.

Now the intercessors are stronger in prayer than the leaders. They start by praying for them but then they begin to assume a ruling function. They are hearing from God and the leaders are hearing from them. They slip from serving to leading and start to usurp the leaders' position.

Intercession is not a ruling function; it is a serving function, a ministry of help intended to hold up the hands of the servants of God not to snatch the rod from them. The only way this situation can be prevented is if the leader doesn't abdicate, but leads from up front. Leadership is hearing God and taking the first step so that others follow you.

When things go wrong

There are people with their own, sometimes subconcious, agenda, looking to control through prayer and intercession. This spirit of control in the spiritual realm is equivalent to witchcraft. It can be subtle but it is also capable of great aggression. There are many reasons why a desire to control might have taken root in a personality but, whatever the reasons may be, this problem has to be seen for what it is and addressed. If it isn't, a God-given ministry can be turned away from holiness and can become an inroad of bondage and destruction.

Let me say quite clearly that intercession has nothing whatsoever to do with control, manipulation or a domineering, ruling spirit. There are those who think they have a God-given right to dominate people. Such 'rights' are not given by God! The only way to deal with the problem is for the leader to confront it quickly.

If you begin to feel intimidated by the outbursts of those who are meant to be supporting you, there's a problem. And you have to have the clarity of sight to see where the problem lies. It's no good trying to take a splinter out of anyone else's eye when there's a plank in your own! It is fundamentally important for us all, especially leaders, to remain in the vine, to have our own very close and personal talk with God.

A dominating spirit will not enjoy the company of others who resist the domination. These will usually end up being dismissed, patronised or rejected. Stunted church growth and division both hatch from this little viper's nest. What began as one of the most beautiful ministries there is can end as one of the most diabolical; debased, utterly spoiled and worse – a vicious weapon in the enemy's hand.

I don't want to leave anyone with the impression that all intercessors are about to take over the church! There are usually just as many problems with leaderships or leaders who are dominating and self-centred and who don't give themselves or anyone else the space and freedom to hear from God for themselves.

What happens when the intercessors are right? Prayer can be a heady thing. You get answers, you get results. People begin to look to you. And perhaps the church leader isn't hearing God at all. But they haven't given up their right to lead the church. What then? A leader must be determined to hear the voice of God and to obey it; to do what is asked because God is asking. You've got to be prepared to accept that voice wherever it comes from (even if it's sister pain-in-the-neck!).

Praying in tongues

The balance between leadership and congregation is vitally important in the use of spirtual gifts. And these gifts, especially the vocal ones, like tongues, can have a prominent part in praying together. Through the influence of the Charismatic movement more and more Christians are practising praying in tongues especially in their own personal devotions. But I don't think that we have yet even begun to understand the power of this gift of the Holy Spirit. There are several different uses of tongues but primarily, it is a prayer language given by God:

'For anyone who speaks in a tongue does not speak to men but to God. Indeed, no one understands him; he utters mysteries with his spirit' (1 Cor 14:2). This should encourage every Christian to seek God for this gift and use it to the full in their prayer life. When praying privately it does not matter that no one understands your prayers in tongues because the Holy Spirit is directing you as you pray not out of your own understanding but out of your spirit. In this way the Holy Spirit helps you to pray well beyond the reach of your natural understanding and in perfect harmony with the will of God.

Using tongues like this in your own private prayer times is one aspect of the use of tongues, but what about praying in tongues in public meetings? This is a subject which often causes much debate and disagreement among Christians. To find our way through this we have to look very carefully at the Apostle Paul's teaching about prophecy and tongues in his letter to the Corinthian church (1 Corinthians 14).

In this church people who had the gift of tongues had evidently been standing up and giving tongues without having what they said interpreted for the church. They were using their gift inappropriately. Paul complains strongly about this: 'I thank God that I speak in tongues more than all of you. But in the church I would rather speak five intelligible words to instruct others than ten thousand words in a tongue' (1 Corinthians 14:18). He states clearly what to do about it: 'If there is no interpreter, the speaker should keep quiet in the church and speak to himself and God' (1 Corinthians 14:28).

This makes perfect sense to me. What good is it to anybody if someone stands up and speaks words that no one else understands? When you address a congregation you are taking the floor, everyone's attention is on you. How selfish to do that and then just to pray in tongues. You're asking for people's attention and then you're denying them meaning; they can't participate. That's not love, that's not corporate praying together or meeting together.

However, it is important to notice that Paul is not rejecting the personal use of tongues in a public meeting. He forbids anyone from addressing the congregation in tongues without there also being an interpretation so that all may understand and be edified. But Paul also establishes the personal use of tongues in the congregational setting by encouraging those who are speaking without interpretation to pray in tongues privately addressing God and not the congregation publicly. 1 Corinthians 14:28 makes this point clearly. The tongues-speaker should be silent in the church if there is no interpreter, that is, they should not address the congregation in tongues. Rather, they should speak to themselves and to God. This personal use of tongues is addressed to God, not to the congregation.

Paul says nothing against corporate speaking in tongues. Rather it is established by the same principles he sets down for individual and personal use of tongues. In this way the entire congregation may pray in tongues together, each one being heard by God in the same way that God hears us when we all pray together. This is a particularly powerful way to pray especially when we all pray together following the prayer line the Holy Spirit has given us for a particular situation.

Paul describes what it must be like for someone who has never met anything like it before to come into a meeting and find people giving one tongue after another with no interpretation. This hapless person's verdict would be, 'You are out of your mind.' I should think it would feel fairly meaningless and time wasting to everybody there, except possibly the speakers.

On the other hand, if someone new comes into a meeting and finds everyone prophesying in turn, this, says Paul, would have a very different effect. When people prophesy, especially in small groups or over particular individuals, God often speaks in a very clear, direct and personal way. Prophecy is God speaking to us. It is in the language of the hearer. The newcomer would understand it straight away and would hear the secrets of his heart laid bare as, one by one, people prophesied. This would cause him to 'fall down and worship God, exclaiming, "God is really among you!"' (1 Corinthians 14:25).

To summarise, Paul is pointing out the beauty of the gift of tongues when used correctly in prayer. This means we can pray in tongues privately in our personal devotions and pray corporately in a public meeting. But in it all, Paul is pointing out the folly of speaking to God when he would rather we listened to him! It's not that praying in tongues is wrong, rather, it can be done inappropriately to the detriment of the hearers.

Targeting issues together

When we are together and praying under a corporate anointing we have usually come knowing what we want to achieve. One person can lead the prayer and every-one else can show their agreement at the end of it by saying 'Amen'. This is usually a quiet form of praying, especially useful in petitionary prayer. It is easily accessible and can be used anywhere.

Another way to pray, which is louder and can be more combative, is when we all raise our voices together in agreement over an issue. We can all pray together at the same time about the same thing. Each of us will see slightly different aspects of it and will pray accordingly and so more can be achieved. This is not nonsensical or a confused cacophany since we know what we're doing; we are aiming our prayer with specific purpose. We are targetting an issue together.

The use of this kind of corporate prayer, and tongues in particular, must be grounded on the principle of love, fellowship and participation. Not everyone has the gift of tongues. We usually offer to pray for anyone who hasn't the gift to receive it, for Paul says, 'I would like every one of you to speak in tongues' (1 Corinthians 14:5). Or we affirm those who don't have the gift and include them. The principle of love says that you don't leave anyone out. Everyone praying together in tongues except those who can't is unbiblical and flouting overriding principles. *Everyone praying* is what we need; then we shall have unity, strength and power.

When we are worshipping together at KT we have moments in the meeting when we might encourage people to pray or sing in tongues all together. But everything must be done in an orderly way and be open to everyone, whatever language they would like to use. When your spirit and the Holy Spirit are together free to praise God openly in a gathering of God's people, the worship can be not only unifying and powerful, but also very beautiful; a pleasing and lovely offering to God.

All the believers spoke and sang the praises of God in new languages at the same time on the day of Pentecost and this is still a valid and orderly expression of our worship together today.

Wednesdays at eight!

All this makes for some of the most exciting and thrilling times we can possibly experience together this side of heaven. We should approach corporate prayer with full anticipation, expecting something to happen. We should be eager to see the great potential of praying together realised. Prayer meetings should be the most powerful and creative meetings in the church's programme. But remember prayer cannot always be programmed. I once saw a poster outside a church advertising a preaching series on prayer which read:

'God Answers Prayer – every Wednesday at eight o'clock'. It looked as if the Lord was unavailable outside 'surgery' hours! The genuine prayer life of a church will include programmed prayer meetings but also spontaneous times of prayer in response to a special need or some clear alert given by the Holy Spirit.

One such time we were given a particular burden to pray for a breakthrough in our church growth strategy. We were at saturation point in our building and yet felt the urgency of the Holy Spirit not to stop reaching out and expanding. But how could we? It was another crucial turning point in our church. The prayer release God gave us could not be contained in the regular 'times of prayer' on the weekly prayer schedule. We called for special periods of prayer: early-morning prayer times, late-night sessions and lunch-time meetings. Also, as people picked up this prayer emphasis, prayer was multiplied through countless small groups all over London and beyond. Individuals would come into the church at all hours of the day and night, whether there was a meeting or not, and pray. Spontaneity was the genuine hallmark of God's working among us. Out of this season of prayer came our church-planting vision, and now some years later we are planting out such new groups at the rate of more than one per month.

We will see later how to encourage such creative prayer strategy in your church or prayer group. But first, let's take a look at the two most important issues confronting praying people today: spiritual warfare and evangelism.

9   Prayer is an Act of War

Woolly wolves and pious ostriches

When learning about spiritual forces, both good and evil, there are two mistakes that people make, to a lesser or greater degree. These two mistakes are so common and can be so disempowering that it is worth mentioning them before we go any further.

The first great mistake is to become fixated on evil, going around looking for it, paranoid, expecting that somehow, someplace, somewhere, the devil is going to get you. You will end up neurotic or worse, imagining demons where there aren't any, living your life defensively, looking for the worst in people, finding the worst in people and producing the worst in people! This mindset is light years away from living in the Spirit of God. 'For God has not given us a spirit of fear but of power and of love and of a sound mind' (2 Timothy 1:7 RSV).

A person who has bought into this brand of defensive thinking is already beaten. If he or she doesn't end up a gibbering wreck, fearful of the world and everything in it, they are in grave danger of fleshing out the stereotypical image of a narrow-minded, joyless, bigotted, critical and judgemental doom merchant: the sort of person who is full of aggressive religious tirades and enjoys nothing more than a good witch-hunt or a spot of scapegoating! But the fruit of the Spirit is 'love, joy, peace, patience, kindness, goodness, faithfulness, gentleness and self-control' (Galatians 5:22–23). I'll leave you to judge whose camp those who are obsessed with negative issues are living in.

The second great mistake is to deny evil all together. Sometimes this happens because a person finds it too threatening. They think they can't cope with it so they would rather not address it at all. Even if that means becoming selectively blind.

At first sight this kind of person seems much more pleasant. He or she may seem outwardly very 'nice' but will inwardly be controlled by all sorts of underlying fears. The central position is, again, defensive. The unreality of such people is usually easy to detect. Among their ranks are those who meet you with fixed smiles, masks that say, 'I'm a joyful, happy, victorious Christian and this smile is going to prove it to you.' There is an element of detachment telling you all the time that, underneath, the reality is very different. Such people are hollow. They are not smiling because they're genuinely interested in you; they're more concerned with how impressed you're going to be with them! Trying to relate in a real and honest way is about as easy as having a relationship with a nodding donkey on an empty oilfield.

Then there are those who react with sudden and unexpected hostility or who swiftly change the subject if you express the mildest negative sentiment about anything. Some people would excuse murder rather than admit culpability over the smallest misdemeanour never mind the largest.

This defensive position can be so entrenched that people start to array barrages of Bible verses to maintain it. In such circumstances anyone with an ounce of discernment is promoted to the office of arch trouble-maker.

Let me tell you something: deception doesn't come from God! It is one of the enemy's commonest weapons. Where it becomes ingrained it damages and distorts people; when it is full blown, it produces hypocrisy. Most unbelievers are more attuned to the truth than this. They see through it and good for them! When the blind try to lead the blind both fall into the pit, as Jesus tells us. We can't bring anyone to God when we're in this state. And that's just how the enemy likes it.

If we are nearing either of these extremes we are operating out of fear and unbelief: fear that Satan is stronger than God after all and unbelief in Christ's victory over him for all time on the cross at Calvary. We become victims, huddled together against the worst, believing ourselves to have no power to change anything. Or we become convinced we have to aggress-ively defend ourselves. This is, indeed, a dark mindset to inhabit. Those who live in this place end up relying on their own human efforts to defeat evil, often not realising their enemy has them already captured.

This is what happens when we try to defend ourselves in the flesh against something which is spiritual. We can't. It's as simple as that. We shall be defeated and conquered every time. Instead of growing in the know-ledge of the truth which sets us free we shall become members of the Church of Defensive Behaviour, a diverted and bound-up people trying to influence others only to further justify ourselves, though we may be under the impression we're holding an outreach.

I think that God sometimes answers our prayers by allowing our efforts to fail. But, always, he is waiting for us to come to him in Spirit and truth and receive his mind on the matter.

I know of a certain church that was once seeking a new building to use as a base for their activities. They were a forward-looking and go-ahead group of people. A local leisure centre came on the market and, driven more by enthusiasm than by inspiration, the church went out and out to acquire it. Urged on by several so-called 'words from the Lord' the leadership persisted in their attempts to negotiate for the building, all without success. Eventually, after much heartache and needless expense, they gave up exhausted. It had been a human desire but not a God directed one.

May we be open for the Spirit of God to blow mightily on us, blasting all strife and deception away. Let's ask him to do it, openly, in our churches. Let's ask him and wait on him. Out with fear, unbelief and ignorance! To fight a spiritual war we need to understand the spiritual terrain. We need spiritual weapons. Now let's go on and discuss what we are about, what our weapons are, how to use them and how to win.

Picnics on the battlefield

When God called us, as a church, to repent of the obstacles that were hindering our prayer life together, one of the first things to go was civilian mentality. This is a legacy of the ostrich approach. It says, 'Leave Satan alone and he'll leave you alone. Live the Christian life and preach the gospel.'

While I am all for living the Christian life and preaching the gospel, we have to understand that the very act of doing that is encroaching on what the enemy sees as his ground. From his point of view and from God's the very breath of prayer is the breath of warfare. The minute we try to pray in the will of God on this earth we are, like it or not, involved in spiritual conflict because 'the reason the Son of God appeared was to destroy the devil's work' (1 John 3:8). And he wants to go on doing it, carrying that victory through into a daily reality. And I'm sure you can understand just how pleased the enemy is about that!

God's Church worldwide is potentially a vast and extremely powerful army. But what has happened to us? There are whole battalions who have forgotten how to fight. And many more never knew in the first place. Some of us don't even believe there's a battle anymore; lulled into a false sense of security or straight unbelief, we have taken off our armour, put down our shields and let our swords go rusty. When you have no armour, what is protecting you? How can you defend yourself with no shield? How do you attack with no sword? You are unguarded, ripe for an enemy take-over.

Too often we have turned the battlefield into a picnic area and let our enemy walk all over us. Scripture tells us that the devil is like a 'roaring lion looking for someone to devour' (1 Peter 5:8). Do you think he's going to be bribed by a cucumber sandwich? We might try to play the civilian with him but he is certainly never going to be civil with us. Love your human enemies, by all means; yes, do good to those who hate you, but don't love the spiritual forces of evil in the heavenly realms. And don't ignore them either. Hate them! Hate what they're doing! Close them down! What alliance can light have with darkness? None. They cannot exist together.

Jesus tells us that we are the light of the world (Matthew 5:14). Are we going to allow the Church, the bride of Christ, to grow dim like a once-bright but now setting sun? Are we going to let darkness overtake us? Heaven forbid!

Finally, be strong in the Lord and in his mighty power. Put on the full armour of God so that you can take your stand against the devil's schemes. For our struggle is not against flesh and blood, but against the rulers, against the authorities, against the powers of this dark world and against the spiritual forces of evil in the heavenly realms. (Ephesians 6:10–12).

Getting personal

At the end of his letter to the church in Ephesus, the Apostle Paul shows us there is a God-ordained way to combat the devil's schemes.

Therefore put on the full armour of God, so that when the day of evil comes, you may be able to stand your ground, and after you have done everything, to stand. Stand firm then, with the belt of truth buckled round your waist, with the breastplate of righteousness in place, and with your feet fitted with the readiness that comes from the gospel of peace. In addition to all this, take up the shield of faith, with which you can extinguish all the flaming arrows of the evil one. Take the helmet of salvation and the sword of the Spirit, which is the word of God. And pray in the Spirit on all occasions with all kinds of prayer and requests. With this in mind, be alert and always keep on praying for all the saints. (Ephesians 6:13–18).

Paul is exhorting us to be ready to fight, ready in every way, with appropriate defences in position and our weaponry ready for the attack. Then he tells us to pray. This is the way to defeat the enemy.

The 'armour of God' represents truths about our

lifestyle, truths that we must appropriate and live in if we are to be victorious. Some people like to mime putting on the armour. This can sometimes be useful as a reminder of your protection and your weaponry but it is important to remember that a mime will never make you a victorious Christian. It is living and operating in these truths that gives us power to win.

When the Apostle Paul wrote this letter to the Ephesians he was imprisoned in Rome. During this time he was, at some point, likely to have been chained to a soldier. The armour described is based on that of a Roman soldier.

Warfare today can be very impersonal. Armies don't even have to see their enemies face to face, but in Paul's day things were very different. A Roman soldier was equipped for hand-to-hand combat. He was part of an army, following orders, moving according to a set strategy and he was ready to fight, man to man. This is his background and, spiritually speaking, it is also ours.

Spiritual warfare is personal. If we take care of our armour and our weapons and pray, then we shall be living in the vine, we shall be at one with the Holy Spirit. When we follow the Spirit's leading then no harm will come to us that God does not allow for his good purposes. We must be steadfast. It is not his will that any of us be overtaken by evil. Instead, he wants to continue the outworking of Satan's defeat at the cross. And he wants to do it through us, his Church!

Sometimes it can look as though a skirmish is lost when a battle is really in the process of being won. Battles need God's strategies and many great victories are won through sacrifice. In fact, the greatest victory ever was won in exactly this way! God's ways are so much deeper than the enemy's. But there are, perhaps, some of us who have lost battles because we haven't undertstood the principles of engagement.

A young graduate was having trouble developing his business. The more he prayed and the harder he worked, the worse the situation became. Convinced that God had led him into computing, he was puzzled as to why it seemed as if it was all going wrong. But then the breakthrough came. He was offered a huge contract with a leading computing company that would have been impossible to take on had his business not slowed down to the extent it had. God had his hand on the situation but the young businessman was totally out of touch with the Spirit's strategy.

It is no use trying to knock down enemy strongholds in prayer when we don't maintain our armour. We are just making ourselves vulnerable to the enemy. Do you think he's going to sit quietly by while we go about taking his territory? Believe me, while he has the chance, he won't waste any time cutting down as many of us as he can manage. Remember, this is personal: it's about your weak spots, it's about your blind spots, it's about your apathy, your ignorance, your sin. I'm not trying to be insulting here, I'm just stating what actually happens.

We have to realise the importance of what we are about and the reality of it. Anyone moving in God is going to be attacked by an enemy who doesn't play fair. In fact, he plays dirty, as dirty as you can get. He is like 'a roaring lion', and if you are caught unawares he will attack your health, your family, your security and your peace of mind. It's time to take a look at how we go about preventing him and how we can successfully close him down.

Spiritual protection: truth and righteousness

Armour is for defence. It is intended to be used in battle. It's no use at all left hanging on the wall as an object to be looked at occasionally and admired. We are talking about something intensely practical. The use of it is the difference between life and death.

The armour of God is to be used – used individually and used corporately in the church. If we are not living faithfully in it then we are vulnerable to enemy attack. If we are not living in it corporately then our church is open to all sorts of inroads from the enemy.

The first piece of armour to be mentioned by Paul is the belt of truth. A love of truth is the starting place. It is a fundamental attitude of heart and mind. What we believe or disbelieve shapes the sort of people we are.

A Roman civilian wore long, flowing robes. Can you imagine getting caught up in a fight wearing those? You would probably trip yourself up before the enemy got anywhere near you. Civilian clothing is just not appropriate. You have to be dressed to fight, ready at all times, with the tunic tightly bound around the waist.

In a spiritual war, truth is not an optional extra. The enemy will use deceit. He will try to make us believe things which aren't true and disbelieve things that are. Be very careful what you believe. The word for truth used here is *aletheia* which means truth as opposed to error. God expects us to hold on to truth, digesting it, making it the basis of our outward and inward stance.

The belt has a strap which supports the sword. Paul describes the sword of the Spirit as the Word of God. There is a close relationship between the belt and the sword. The Word of God, which is truth, is the sword. If you want to be effective in using it then you must have great regard for truth, must not only know it but be rooted in it. Your ability to fight depends upon it. Your survival depends upon it.

Some people may preach the Word of God and be successful from a public preformance point of view, but if they are not saturated privately in that truth then they are giving the enemy an open invitation to trip them up in full view of that same public, causing disillusionment and discouragement for many, and holding the Lord up to ridicule. A total triumph for the enemy! Wear your belt of truth with integrity.

A Roman breastplate was made in two ways; either it was metal moulded to fit the soldier's neck and torso, or it was of linen which had been covered with protective strips of animal horn. A breastplate gave protection to the vital organs, the neck, torso and the jugular vein.

Righteousness is as important to us in a spiritual war as a breastplate was for a Roman soldier in battle. If we do not have it then it is as if our whole chest, including our heart and lungs, is openly exposed to the enemy. Serious injury or death will surely follow, and quickly! 'Above all else, guard your heart, for it is the wellspring of life' (Proverbs 4:23).

Since righteousness is so important let's remind ourselves of what is meant by it. Righteousness in the New Testament refers to both imputed and practical righteousness. Imputed righteousness is the free gift of God that comes through faith in Christ. It is the righteousness won for us by Jesus who paid the just penalty for our evil.

Practical righteousness is the practical outworking of our position in Christ, as enabled by the Holy Spirit. To put it simply, it is thinking and doing good and not evil.

To be fully protected we must be right with God by both standing in faith and walking in obedience. We need to know that we have perfect righteousness before God in Christ Jesus so that we can come to him in faith, but we also have to walk before him in confession and repentance. Or, to go back to our former analogy, we must take a bath and then keep on washing our feet as often as they need it!

'For from within, out of men's hearts, come evil thoughts, sexual immorality, theft, murder, adultery, greed, malice, deceit, lewdness, envy, arrogance and folly' (Mark 7:21).

We don't have to become obsessively concerned with our imperfections but it is, nevertheless, very important for us to regularly check our hearts to ensure that our motivations are right. Ask the Holy Spirit to shine his light, to reveal to you any unrighteousness. And don't turn away your head when he shines that light into dark corners! Look at what he's showing you. Go straight to Jesus, talk it over with him, confess it and repent of it. Let him wash your feet. Then turn right round and go in the opposite direction.

Spiritual protection: peace and faith

A Roman soldier's feet needed strong, sturdy protection from rough terrain. His shoes were heavy, leather sandals with thick, studded soles, heavily and securely strapped around feet and legs to well above the ankles. They enabled feet to grip the ground, lending stability and surefootedness for running and fighting.

How does this apply to us? We have to be able to take our 'stand against the devil's schemes' (Ephesians 6:11). Standing on the gospel of peace will give us the ability to manoeuvre ourselves into whatever position is advantageous to the Lord, and to stand in his protection, his peace and his strength, surefooted and immovable. The gospel of peace, far from bringing hatred and human warfare, actually ushers in reconciliation.

All this is from God, who reconciled us to himself in Christ and gave us the ministry of reconciliation: that God was reconciling the world to himself in Christ, not counting men's sins against them. And he has committed to us the message of reconciliation (2 Corinthians 5:18–19).

Our stance here must be strong yet full of peace. We are to be immovable, 'as shrewd as snakes' and, at the same time, 'as innocent as doves' (Matthew 10:16). 'Be on your guard; stand firm in the faith; be men of courage; be strong. Do everything in love' (1 Corinthians 16:13).

Now to our shield. Roman soldiers used two kinds, a smaller, round one designed to fend off blows when fighting with a sword or a spear and a very large, curved one which could totally protect the whole body. This was made of layered wood and covered with leather treated especially to extinguish the burning pitch on the tips of enemy arrows.

Most of us will have had some experience of the fiery arrows of the evil one. Whether they are harmful words, acts, situations or temptations, they are characterised by a particular intensity and the smouldering, spreading, destructive agony they bring in their wake. They can be, for a time, totally debilitating. We can just do without it! Faith is the shield that can protect us here. And it can protect us from every single flaming arrow.

The minute we begin a relationship with God we become aware of him speaking to us; we learn about his character through his written Word – the Word that is general and applicable to everyone. We each hear from him in a more specific way too in words that are about and just for us. These words, this communication between ourselves and our God, will form for us an impenetrable shield, but this depends on us taking God at his Word, believing him and trusting him. Then when the enemy comes at us in a particularly vicious way we can stand firm and at peace; the faith in our hearts based on God's Word to us forms a barrier of protection around us.

One way that Roman soldiers used to protect themselves was by standing together and boxing themselves in with their shields. These large shields would be held around the edge of the 'box' and the soldiers in the middle would hold their shields to face the sky so that all the people involved were totally covered. Nothing unexpected could drop down from the sky and injure anyone. And the soldiers could march wherever they wanted.

This is a picture of an invaluable spiritual defensive technique. As a body of people (and all the instructions in the last chapter of Ephesians were to a body of Christians, the church at Ephesus), we must watch over each other in prayer, reminding each other of God's promises, 'covering' each other with our faith as we would if we were fighting with shields. This is a powerful way to prevent what could otherwise be devastating enemy attacks. 'Every word of God is flawless; he is a shield to those who take refuge in him' (Proverbs 30:5).

I remember a Christian minister whose daughter had been born with a rare condition affecting several faculties. The medical prognosis was uncertain and discouraging. Both he and his wife came from large families whose members were nearly all committed Christians. Like a shield they enclosed them in prayer. Several churches too were alerted and began to pray. The affirmation this gave to the young couple with their baby was deeply encouraging. Years later that child has developed practically normally in every faculty contrary to all medical expectations.

Salvation and the Word of God

The last piece of armour that Paul mentions is the helmet. A Roman helmet was made either of strong leather covered with metal or of cast metal with leather cheek pieces. These helmets were strong enough to take the blows from heavy broadswords which would penetrate an unprotected skull.

Spiritually speaking, the helmet protects the mind. It stands for the knowledge that we have a relationship with God, through Jesus, his Son. And we know that, if we do not turn away, salvation is ours. Hope, encouragement and perseverence are what God is giving us here. And what do these qualities protect us from?

The broadsword of the enemy is a poleaxing doubt, deep discouragement and despondency and the lie that it's futile to carry on. One well-timed swipe with a penetrating dose of any of this nasty little cocktail would be enough to cause anyone to stagger and fall.

Keep your helmet of salvation on. Don't allow your mind to grow vulnerable to Satan's lies. Don't digest them, don't even let him feed them to you. Fight back straight away! So much spiritual weakness and mental ill-health stems from believing and operating out of lies which have been received as truth. It is vital that we know the difference. Meditate on God's truth and believe him above circumstances, above the opinions of others, above everything. Jesus tells us 'Heaven and earth will pass away, but my words will never pass away' (Luke 21:33). Hope in God and never give up!

'We have this hope as an anchor for the soul, firm and secure. It enters the inner sanctuary behind the curtain' (Hebrews 6:19).

'But since we belong to the day, let us be self-controlled, putting on faith and love as a breastplate, and the hope of salvation as a helmet. For God did not appoint us to suffer wrath but to receive salvation through our Lord Jesus Christ' (1 Thessalonians 5:8–9).

Turning the tables

We have, so far, discussed our defences. What of our weapons of attack? We have one extremely powerful, offensive weapon. Paul describes it as the sword of the Spirit.

The analogy here is with a Roman short sword or dagger, the gladius. This was a two-edged sword about sixty centimetres long. It was used in hand-to-hand combat and was the powerful, precise weapon of a skilled fighter.

The Word of God is the sword of the Spirit and it is a powerful, razor-sharp, cleaving weapon capable of laying bare the enemy's strategies and utterly defeating him.

For the word of God is living and active. Sharper than any double-edged sword, it penetrates even to dividing soul and spirit, joints and marrow; it judges the thoughts and attitudes of the heart. Nothing in all creation is hidden from God's sight. Everything is uncovered and laid bare before the eyes of him to whom we must give account (Hebrews 3:12–13).

The sword of the Spirit is not the general Word of God (*logos*). When we use it in attack it is the specific word of God for a particular situation or person, a *rhema* word which is living, active and spiritually charged for a specific purpose.

The best example in Scripture of this usage is when Jesus confronted the devil in the wilderness. The devil came to trip Jesus up before he even began his ministry on the earth. Jesus had spent forty days and nights praying and fasting. If he had lost this battle there would have been no salvation for any of us. Satan would have won. Yet the temptations were very real. The devil tried to overcome Jesus by appealing to his physical craving for food. Then he tried to get him to put God to the test, which would have caused him to sin and invalidated his mission. When this failed he tried to bribe Jesus to worship him by offering all the beauty, glory and earthly power of the world in return.

At each exchange Jesus defeated the enemy with God's word, the sword of the Spirit. His use of Scripture was specifically and accurately targetted and demolished the enemy's attack. He countered each temptation with 'It is written .... ' Jesus knew the word of God and used it. When the enemy comes to us whispering his deceits and accusations we can respond, 'But God says .... ' In warfaring situations we can ask God for a specific word with which to fight. At his word Satan trembles.

No running away

The first thing to remember is that we must face the enemy. We don't want to be binding devils at the breakfast table while everyone else is saying grace, but we need to be aware of the realities. Don't be ignorant of the enemy's schemes. The Roman breastplate had no back to it. A Roman soldier who turned and ran in battle risked serious injury, if not loss of life. If you try to hide and avoid spiritual conflict you are already defeated.

The second thing to bear in mind is this; the weapons of the enemy are limited. They are very varied in application but they rely on two basic principles for their success: deceit and accusation.

I have already said a lot about how to deal with accusation. We take a bath, we have our feet washed and what is there left to accuse us of? Look carefully at guilt. Ask the Spirit to show you if it is real guilt as a result of your own wrong-doing; perhaps you haven't tried to put a matter right; perhaps you need to appologise to someone.

If you haven't offended against God or your neighbour then you could be suffering because you haven't come up to someone else's standards. This is false guilt. Perhaps you're not the person someone else wants you to be. Perhaps you're not fulfilling a role they are forcing you to take. If this is the case then, quite honestly, it's their problem not yours. You need to know how far to go in accommodating people. Jesus said we were to go the extra mile not the extra transglobal marathon. Don't be deceived into becoming the worm. And don't be deceived into becoming the tyrant either, trying to keep other people dancing on your strings 'for their own good'.

One thing I have learned about the enemy is that he is a robber and a spoiler. The Church of God has been robbed and spoiled for long enough! We all need to ask God for discernment; we all need to go about cultivating clear sight. Then we can see how and why the enemy has infiltrated. This may involve us in all sorts of prayer, not only warfare. We may need to intercede for people. We may need to pray for their healing. We may need to 'cover' them in prayer. We may be involved in Christ's ministry of reconciliation. Determine to stay alert and ready.

Our authority is in Jesus

The Old Testament was written to be a record of God's dealing with his people that would serve as a warning and example to us all. In it we can find many examples of God going to war against his enemies.

'The Amalekites came and attacked the Israelites at Rephidim ... The Lord will be at war against the Amalekites from generation to generation' (Exodus 17:8, 16).

This whole passage in Exodus is full of warfare language. The picture is for us – now. In the same way that the Israelites' enemies stood against them and attacked them while they sought to lay hold of God's promises, the devil and his minions will oppose us as we seek to pray the promises of God into being. He hates the thought of God's will being done on earth as it is in heaven and he will seek to defeat us by any means available. But, do not fear. A great victory has already been won. We can learn how to appropriate it. Today our battle is spiritual and not against flesh and blood, but these Old Testament examples of physical battles are just as relevant to us. They are demonstrating spiritual principles that we need to know.

God has a unique strategy for each battle and will give us specific instructions. 'Moses said to Joshua, "Choose some of our men and go out to fight the Amalekites. Tomorrow I will stand on top of the hill with the staff of God in my hands"' (Exodus 17:9).

Not all of God's strategies were militarily sound!

Moses stands on top of a hill holding up the Rod of God, Joshua circles Jericho and sends shock waves through all the resident armies in the promised land. It seems there is no set or predictable way of winning.

Exactly the same is true of the battles we find ourselves in today. It is absolutely essential that we get our battle plans from the Lord and that we don't move unless he has directed us. We must be sensitive to the leading of his Spirit; presumption can be very dangerous in spiritual warfare. Satan will tempt us, as he did Jesus, to prove we are heirs of God and to demonstrate our authority over him. The minute we step out of the will of God and try to confront him in our own strength he will wipe us out.

Moses' rod was a symbol of his authority. The staff represents his calling but Moses had to lay it down before he could take it up properly. It was only known as the Rod of God after he had thrown it down; then it had worked miracles. Moses had to lay his life down and no longer try to do things his way but yield to the plan and direction of God. He found his true authority only when he laid down his striving and exchanged trusting in his own abilities for trusting in the call of God for his life.

Our authority does not come from who we are but from the fact we are covenant heirs and sons of God. And we are only this because of Jesus. 'All authority in heaven and on earth has been given to me' Jesus tells us (Matthew 28:18). And because of this, if we are living in the vine, the same authority belongs to us.

'He who listens to you listens to me; he who rejects you rejects me; but he who rejects me rejects him who sent me.'

The seventy-two returned with joy and said, 'Lord, even the demons submit to us in your name.'

He replied, 'I saw Satan fall like lightning from

heaven. I have given you authority to trample on snakes and scorpions and to overcome all the power of the enemy; nothing will harm you. However, do not rejoice that the spirits submit to you, but rejoice that your names are written in heaven' (Luke 10:16–20).

Jesus says, 'I will give you the keys of the kingdom of heaven; whatever you bind on earth will be bound in heaven, and whatever you loose on earth will be loosed in heaven' (Matthew:16:19). Jesus has given us access to great power but to receive it we must live in submission to him and use it in his name. All spiritual authority must be in submission; this is a scriptural principle that was true even of Jesus. He partook of and expressed his Father's authority because he was completely submitted to his Father. The humility that exists in the Godhead is the ultimate linking of power with submission. Where there is no submission there is no authority.

An advancing army

We are a people who are living in the benefits of the victory at Calvary. There Jesus disarmed every power and principality and was raised far above them in the heavenly places (Ephesians 1 and 2). We are now new creations raised with Christ and in him are a little higher than the angels with his delegated power and authority. So, although we ourselves have no power to rebuke spiritual forces (if we rebuke them they will rebuke us [Acts 19:15]), we have received that power in Christ and, as his representatives on earth, anointed and empowered by the Holy Spirit, we can say, 'In the name of Jesus I rebuke you.' We must not be intimidated but fully aware of our position in Christ if we are to be effective in the place of warfare.

There is one other thing that we must be to be effective and that is – together! As individuals we are like lone snipers, picking off enemy forces here and there. A lone sniper would be very ill-advised to launch a solo attack on a battalion, wouldn't he? The same is true in the spiritual realm and the consequences might not be dissimilar. This lesson was brought home very sharply to me not long after I had become a Christian.

It would have been 1972. Every day I walked to the underground train station and I always passed a particular house in London's West Kensington. It was the home of a mystical cult that was, at the time, gaining in popularity. Each time I passed it I was aware of how demonic the place was, yet more and more people seemed to be being sucked in.

At last I started to take authority over what was going on. And I did it every day as I passed. It seemed good and right in God.

After a few weeks of this I was beginning to grow increasingly discouraged. I didn't link the depression with the praying at all. It got worse and worse. Finally I was in such a state that I was even thinking there was no point in being a Christian. Then I asked someone for prayer.

The person who prayed for me had a word of knowledge telling me what had caused the trouble and a word of wisdom to let me know what the Lord wanted me to do about it.

'It's that house,' she said, 'the one you keep praying for. The Lord is asking you to stop praying and to commit it into his hands.'

I did this and the depression lifted. Even more amazingly, within three weeks the cult left and the house was clear! That taught me a lot about the overall sovereignty of God. Constant aggressive confrontation of the enemy cannot always be right. There are situations where we are too unprotected, too vulnerable.

When we move together our power and protection are multiplied; we can achieve so much more. Instead of having to back off we can advance and conquer. God intends us all to have a place somewhere in his army. To go on the offensive will often mean that we first have to deal with the 'strong man' in the heavenlies. This can be done in intercessory and warfare prayer. When we are living our armoured lifestyle and praying together, strongholds can, indeed, be bound and then houses subsequently plundered. But it takes team work.

Moses, Aaron, Hur and Joshua worked together to defeat the Amalekites. Joshua took the troops and fought. Moses held up the Rod of God. Aaron and Hur supported him. There was no arguing over who would hold the Rod, no bickering over who would support Moses and who would fight. There was no division, no competition, no rivalry; such fleshly pursuits didn't enter into it. That unity was the difference between victory and defeat.

Whatever happens, conduct yourselves in a manner worthy of the gospel of Christ. Then, whether I come and see you or only hear about you in my absence, I will know that you stand firm in one spirit, contending as one man for the faith of the gospel (Philippians 1:27).

Spiritual warfare is tough work. Those at the front line don't need you to try and replace them. They don't need you to envy them. They don't need you to be threatened by them or to compete with them in any way. They need your support and expression of unity. If you are not united with your brothers and sisters then you have no chance against the enemy.

Unity is expressing agreement in spirit and it is a bond of peace. It is *not* uniformity. We are all parts of the same body but we are *different* parts. We must encourage each other in our uniqueness; in fact, celebrate it! Unity is not just being friends, though friendship is important. Unity is not being nice, warm and genial with one another. We must start to see things in perspective. In a war you don't even have to like each other to fight together!

Unseen realms

Two thousand years ago Jesus Christ defeated Satan at the cross. He has been conquered but we are still fighting him. Why? This is because Satan is defeated but not yet finally bound. Scripture makes it clear that the time for his utter destruction will come but we are now living in an interim period. When God calls us we can, through the Spirit of Christ within us, bind 'strong men'. Together we can smash enemy strongholds. We can do damage to Satan's kingdom and usher in God's glory.

We are called to exercise the authority of Christ, an authority greater than angels or arch angels. When churches are in the flow of the Holy Spirit and acting under the anointing of the Spirit I believe we shall confront and bind spiritual rulers. But this must be done together and at the Lord's command.

In the book fo Daniel we are given some very unusual glimpses of the operation of the spiritual realm and how it is influenced by our prayers. Daniel, by prayer and fasting before God, sought to understand a vision that he had. God sent a powerful angel to meet with him and explain the meaning of the vision but the angel was delayed. The reason for the delay was a being described in Scripture as 'the prince of Persia'.

Daniel persevered in prayer and, finally, the angel reached him, appearing as he was standing on the banks of the Tigris. Daniel reports that only he saw the angel though his companions must have sensed something very awe-inspiring because they were filled with terror and ran to hide themselves.

Daniel's description of the angel is vivid. I wonder how you or I might react coming face to face with a being like this:

A man, dressed in linen, with a belt of the finest gold round his waist. [So far so good. Read on.] His body was like chrysolite [yellow or green precious olivine], his face like lightning, his eyes like flaming torches, his arms and legs like the gleam of burnished bronze, and his voice like the sound of a multitude (Daniel 10:5–6).

The angel goes on to explain why the answer to Daniel's prayer had taken so long.

Do not be afraid, Daniel. Since the first day that you set your mind to gain understanding and to humble yourself before your God, your words were heard, and I have come in response to them. But the prince of the Persian kingdom resisted me twenty-one days. Then Michael, one of the chief princes, came to help me, because I was detained there with the king of Persia. Now I have come to explain to you what will happen to your people in the future (Daniel 10:12–14).

There are three key points here. First, demonic beings (here called princes) not only exist but also try to oppose the operation of God. Some people argue that the prince of Persia was a man and not a spiritual being. What man could have held out against this angel? He was so awesome that Daniel hardly had the strength to speak to him; Daniel's companions ran away from his presence even though they saw nothing. This 'man' is not only supposed to have resisted the angel, but to have done so for twenty-one days. No. What we have here is a spiritual battle: the angel of God is sent to meet the man of God and is opposed by a wicked prince demon.

The second point that concerns us now is that these demonic princes are associated with particular spatial and temporal areas. The prince here was associated with the kingdom of Persia. He was a ruling spirit linked with that kingdom.

Thirdly, and very importantly, here we can clearly see a link between heavenly and earthly activity. What happens in the earth affects what is happening in the heavens and vice versa. By his prayers and persistence Daniel achieved a breakthrough.

On to victory!

The fact that Daniel did not personally address the powers and principalities and saw nothing of the battle itself is sometimes used to deny the need for conscious, personal and aggressive spiritual warfare. This argument considers addressing demonic powers to be wrong and uses a scripture from Zechariah for support – this is where Joshua is standing before the angel of the Lord and Satan is standing ready to accuse him. Here, the angel of the Lord does not personally rebuke the accuser but says, 'The Lord rebuke you, Satan!' (Zechariah 3:2).

To understand these things we have to put them into context. Daniel lived in Old Testament times. He did not have New Testament authority. Jesus had not yet been born let alone sacrificed for the sins of mankind. Neither Daniel nor the angel in the third chapter of Zechariah had the knowledge or the right to use the name of Jesus. Daniel was, in this sense, earthbound.

We are now living in all the benefits of Christ's victory at Calvary. Filled with the Holy Spirit, we can take our place in the heavens, sitting with Christ. And in him we can take authority over the principalities and powers. Jesus taught his disciples that it was necessary to first bind the strong man (demonic forces) neutralising them before releasing those who were held captive; in fact, it is this that he describes as being a proof of the coming of the kingdom of God. 'If I drive out demons by the Spirit of God, then the kingdom of God has come upon you' (Matthew 12:28).

There are numerous examples in Scripture of Jesus personally addressing spiritual forces. During the temptations in the wilderness he rebuffs Satan with his words (Luke 4). When he tells Peter that he is to face suffering and death Peter exclaims, 'Never, Lord! This shall never happen to you!' (Matthew 16:22). Jesus' response is to discern and address the demonic power influencing Peter at that time: 'Get behind me Satan! You are a stumbling block to me; you do not have in mind the things of God, but the things of men' (Matthew 16:23). When Jesus tried to cross the Sea of Galilee and was opposed by the enemy who caused a storm, he rebuked it (Luke 8:25).

In these and many other instances Jesus did not converse and reason with the devil but parried and commanded him. And so can we, although our struggle will be with lesser spiritual forces; rarely, if ever, will we come into direct contact with Satan himself. We can fight against demons in people or enter a level where we are confronting principalities over nations and situations. But for this we must have God's strategy and not take one step outside it. Never, never be presumptuous. Everything must be specifically directed by the Holy Spirit. Magic formulas don't exist. Every battle is different and a strategy will only be effective if God tells you to do it.

For instance, we know that the enemy hates to hear us praising God, but praise is only effective in warfare when it is part of an overall strategy. It isn't necessarily effective just in itself. Battle tactics are situation specific.

Dirty Harry tactics

Satan's basic weapons are twofold: accusation and deception; but his tactics are numerous. Just watch what happens when a church gives itself fully to the work of evangelism. Spiritual oppression, sickness, disunity and often, a whole lot more, are thrown at the fellowship. One church with a desire to reach Cantonese speakers in London entered Chinatown to share the gospel message with those who gathered in the streets, shops and restaurants. The first time the outreach team attempted this kind of evangelism there were significant results with people even being healed on the street. But the next time it was different. Most of the team members felt physically sick and one even vomited. It was an out and out spiritual attack. However they regrouped and gave more time to serious spiritual warfare preparing with more prayer and fasting than before. Soon their victory became apparent with even some gangsters affected by the message.

One favourite tactic of the devil is to set Christians against each other. Armed with the enemy's weapon of accusation many Christians engage the fire power of slander and criticism. It is just as bad wherever it happens but it seems more perverse when Christian leaders come under such attack, and even worse still when leaders attack one another. Denunciations fly from pulpit and page like ballistic missiles aimed at the doctrine, integrity and even the style of other people's ministry. Then the smearing spreads through guilt by association and trial by video, out-of-context quotes and second-hand reports.

It is all covered with a veneer of self-righteous indignation by these self-appointed spiritual watchdogs. In fact these are the devil's bloodhounds sniffing out those who are being effective for God and going in for the easy kill of character assassination. I hardly know of one national or international minister being significantly used of God who is not at this very time fighting needless battles of defence against other Christians' attacks. Satan's tactics must be identified and countered with our own attacks on his kingdom. United prayer offered in love followed by biblical up-building will do it every time.

The Israelites won a great victory at Jericho but they suffered a terrible defeat at Ai where they were just a handful of people going into a city. Here they attacked without the Lord's command or blessing. One of them had sinned before the Lord and the sin had made the whole group 'liable to destruction' (Joshua 7:12). Israel was humiliated, some of her men were killed and courage evaporated. God will not overlook sin. Only after his people had humbled themselves and addressed the sin did he give them plans for victory at Ai.

Much better to seek God first and have a resounding victory than to seek him in tears and agony of heart after you've gone ahead in the flesh and suffered a catastrophic defeat. When we are spending time with Christ in the place of prayer we shall have his heart and mind. When we seek to implement his strategies we need not fear. Then we can go to war with an attitude of accomplished victory, not struggle or defeat. We may still have to fight but we shall win!

10 Dynamic Evangelism

Bomb-making

We may have a tremendously large bomb but, without
a detonator, we cannot access its power. We may have
a crate of detonators but without any dynamite they,
too, are utterly ineffective. We may have a bomb and a
detonator but no one to position it. We want to end up
destroying obstacles; we want to be spiritual dam-
busters, freeing pathways for the flow of the Spirit of
God, not suicide bombers descending indiscriminately
on inappropriate targets and destroying ourselves and
others in the process.

We have talked about the power of God and how to
appropriate that power. We have talked about seeking
him, hearing from him and receiving his strategies. All
of this must have its outworking in action.

Prayer and evangelism is a dynamic combination.
We are going to look now at the nitty gritty of
producing an explosion. We are not just moving in
heavenly places, seeing those bowls of incense rising
before the Father's throne. We are here, living in time,
in the years that have been allotted to us. And round
about us are neighbours, relatives, friends, individual
people that Jesus died for. He wants to give them life
and so do we. But how?

The New Testament is full of commands to go and preach the gospel. If we just pray and don't preach, we are not using God's methods. But, you may say, the ground is so hard, hearts are so cold, we get little or no response. Have you ever thought the fault may lie in the way we pray and the way we preach?

I believe there are very few people who would not accept Jesus Christ. With the right kind of prayer, backing and presentation of the gospel, very few would walk away because it's such a good offer! The main reason people reject it is because they're not ready: the ground isn't prepared and there are spiritual forces that are involved in blinding them.

And even if our gospel is veiled, it is veiled to those who are perishing. The god of this age has blinded the minds of unbelievers so that they cannot see the light of the gospel of the glory of Christ, who is the image of God. For we do not preach ourselves, but Jesus Christ is Lord, and ourselves as your servants for Jesus' sake. For God, who said, 'Let light shine out of darkness' made His light shine in our hearts to give us the light of the knowledge of the glory of God in the face of Christ (2 Corinthians 3–6).

These verses should give us all tremendous hope for those who don't yet know the Lord. It tells us that unbelievers cannot see the light of the gospel. It's not that they refuse to, or that they reject it or that they just will not. They actually cannot see.

That's really good news because we were all just the same weren't we? No one is born into the kingdom of God, naturally speaking. We were all born into this world with a bias to sin. We were all spiritually blind once. But the God who said, 'Let light shine out of darkness' made his light shine in our hearts even when we were blind and dead in our sinful nature.

The miracle of salvation is that God brings his life-giving word and creates life. That's the context here; it's a description of creation. Just as God said, 'Let there be light,' and there was light, so he can speak the light of his revelation into everyone. Yes, including the person who is the most hardened sinner, the very one you would think could never be saved: he is no more lost than you or I once were.

So we are not talking here about trying naturally to persuade people to believe something they don't want to believe, or trying to impress them with our spirituality or anything like that. We must break down this resistance in prayer.

Praying for the unsaved

When we come to pray for the unsaved we are not in any way to be manipulating or controlling in what we think or say. People must stand and be allowed to stand according to their own consciences. Our responsibility is to pray and present the gospel. As I've said before, if you start trying to control people in and through intercession then you are getting into the spirit of witchcraft.

> Therefore, since through God's mercy we have this ministry, we do not lose heart. Rather, we have renounced secret and shameful ways; we do not use deception, nor do we distort the word of God. On the contrary, by setting forth the truth plainly we commend ourselves to every man's conscience in the sight of God. (2 Corinthians 4:1–2.)

The resistance is a supernatural force operating against people. It is this force that we have the authority to deal with because we have authority over the works of Satan. Jesus has given us authority to trample on serpents and scorpions and over all the power of the enemy. We have already seen that our battle is not against flesh and blood but against the principalities and powers, against spiritual wickedness in high places; that is just as true of your next-door neighbour as it is of demonic spirits influencing whole cities or nations.

There are many who have been praying for specific people for a long time not realising that warfare is involved here. People are in the grip of forces that are blinding them and seeking to keep them from the gospel. As well as praying for the individual to have an openness and responsiveness we must pray against these spiritual forces. Then blind eyes shall see.

One man had been coming to our meetings for many years but had never committed his life to Christ in response to the challenge of the gospel. Fred seemed incapable of even absorbing the basic facts of the Christian message. Although he appeared willing to receive Christ, something was holding him back. Then a visiting minister who had been used a great deal by God in setting people free from demonic powers discerned that Fred was bound by such powers. As soon as the minister broke the demonic hold over Fred's life in the name of Jesus he cried out for the Lord to save him from his sins.

The power of the blood of Christ

We begin by pleading the blood of Christ. What does that mean? Let me explain.

Throughout the Old Testament Israel was commanded by God to offer sacrifices to atone for their sins. Jesus became the ultimate sin offering, a sacrifice offered to atone for the sins of the world. He did not merely provide a covering for our sins, but he became 'the Lamb of God, who takes away the sin of the world' (John 1:29). Jesus is the mediator between God and us; his sacrifice was made once for all of us and has forged a path of forgiveness and reconciliation between ourselves and our creator. Justice is part of the nature of God. He can't just forget about sins and pretend they never happened. But now he takes the sinless record of Jesus and he accredits it to us. When he looks at us, we are 'hidden' by Jesus. Jesus has paid the penalty of death for our sin and his life has become our life.

> You have come to God, the judge of all men, to the spirits of righteous men made perfect, to Jesus the mediator of a new covenant, and to the sprinkled blood that speaks a better word than the blood of Abel (Hebrews 12:24).

This verse reminds us that we have come to Jesus and to his sprinkled blood. It goes on to say that this blood speaks. When Cain killed his brother, Abel, he tried to hide it from God but Abel's blood cried out from the ground. God was fully aware of the murder. In this verse we are told that Jesus' blood also speaks and it speaks a better word than the blood of Abel.

Blood in Scripture is symbolic of life violently terminated. Abel's blood was speaking of murder and vengeance but the blood of Christ, shed for all nations, speaks of mercy and forgiveness. 'You are my Son, today I have become your Father. Ask of me and I will make the nations your inheritance, the ends of the earth your possession' (Psalm 2:7–8). Jesus died for the nations; they already belong to him. He is now in the presence of the Father; his blood is, as it were, speaking before the Father's throne, pleading mercy, forgiveness and blessing for the world.

This was really brought home to me a few years ago when I visited Sao Paulo in Brazil. When I was a very young Christian, in fact, just a few months after I was born again, God showed me that I would be going to South America. I kept that in my heart and in prayer for nineteen years. Then God called me. When I was given the invitation the Holy Spirit came upon me and I nearly fell down under the power of God. I knew it was time to go.

When I got there I spent one of the worst days of my entire life in my hotel room. I was almost completely overcome by what began as intercession but developed into intense spiritual confrontation and warfare; it was as if the ruling principalities were right in that hotel room. I was so overcome I didn't even have the energy to pick up the phone and call others to come and pray with me in the struggle. It was like a kind of Gethsemane to me. I felt almost physically pushed around that hotel room by a very strong demonic force as I interceded for the city.

Then I had a beautiful vision. I saw the skyline of Sao Paulo. The blood of Jesus was moving right across the city. I felt the Holy Spirit say to my heart, 'This has been called a city of bloodshed but there is a greater blood that cries greater things than the blood that has been shed here and because of that blood I am going to visit this city in revival.' Then he showed me where it was going to begin – among the poor people on the streets. The intellectuals from the universities would come and study what was happening and then they were going to be blessed and converted. Both the very rich and the poor would come to God. The whole move of God was going to depend on the powerful, sustained and united intercession of Christ's body. But God's desire was that the revival should touch the whole city. That's one of the largest cities in the world, with up to 20 million people living in and around it. All those wonderful people and for every one of them Jesus shed his blood.

So when I pray for someone I can start by knowing that Christ's blood pleads for this person and that I can plead to God along with the blood. I can say, 'Lord Jesus, you have died for this person; there's no reason in heaven or hell why this person should go anywhere other than to be with you.'

Come Holy Spirit!

As soon as you come before the Father's throne in intercession you can say, 'Look, Father, look at Jesus' blood shed for all of us. Do not withhold your grace and mercy from this nation, from this individual.' As soon as you do this you release the Holy Spirit.

> I tell you the truth, it is for your good that I am going away. Unless I go away, the Counsellor will not come to you; but if I go, I will send him to you. When he comes, he will convict the world of guilt in regard to sin and righteousness and judgement (John 16:7–8).

'Going away' for Jesus meant going via the cross and it is because of Jesus' sacrifice that the Holy Spirit can come to us.

Christians talk about the Holy Spirit coming upon the Church but they often forget there is another outpouring of God's Holy Spirit that has been equally purchased by Jesus: the outpouring of the Holy Spirit in conviction upon the world.

When we pray for anyone who's in the world we can call for the Holy Spirit, we can say, 'Father, because of the blood of Jesus, send the Holy Spirit to bring conviction of sin, righteousness and judgement!' That is a powerful operation of the Holy Spirit that, by the grace of God, belongs to everyone in the world, Christian or not – in fact, it's specifically for non-Christians.

So now we are starting to see a progression in the way we can pray: Jesus' blood is shed for this particular person and because of that the Holy Spirit is outpoured for them; when the Holy Spirit is present he will begin to convince and convict.

We must be sent

Everyone who calls on the name of the Lord will be saved. How, then, can they call on the one they have not believed in? And how can they believe in the one of whom they have not heard? And how can they hear without someone preaching to them? And how can they preach unless they are sent? (Romans 10:13–15).

How do we preach? This passage of Scripture makes us aware of the need for a clear presentation of the gospel. It also tells us that we must be sent. People are not going to flock to Christ just because we stand up and start preaching. In fact, in today's spiritual climate, they are more likely to cross over to the other side of the street.

We have seen that everything we do must be soaked in prayer to be effective. The ground must be prepared. We may have to be sensitive to how God wants to prepare a person, how he wants us to speak with them, if and when he wants us to share the gospel. Yes, if.

There are times when it is inappropriate because a person's heart is not yet ready to receive.

Some people interpret 'go and make disciples of all nations' (Matthew 28:19) as 'go and brow-beat all nations into accepting Christ.' Did Jesus ever behave like that? Of course not! This is not the strategy of the Holy Spirit, it is the tactic of the enemy, and this behaviour is light years away from moving in the grace and the power of God. It reminds me of certain church functions I've been to where one has the uncomfortable feeling of being hunted. People come up to you with their predatory smiles. It's truly horrible – in our eyes and in God's. Others may force their message onto the world. But the way of Christ is the way of love, not coercion.

Some people are caught up in the idea that unless you're constantly talking about God you're not serving him. Be very wary of this religious spirit. Remember that Jesus came to serve not to Bible-bash people. Any influence that pressurises or compels you to behave like this has more to do with 'religion' than faith.

Religion is the worst of all human inventions. Satan uses it now just as he did in Jesus' day (remember, Jesus called the religious teachers of his time a 'brood of vipers'). Religion so often becomes a haven of self-righteousness, pride and arrogance of the worst kind, spawning all kinds of evil. It really isn't any excuse to say, 'Ah, but they think they're doing the right thing.' So did Hitler. We have to be very careful to keep our priorities right, to always live in the vine. If we don't, then we too are quite capable of being deceived by the lies of the enemy. Religious deception causes a great deal of damage to people.

Religious form without power

Wars have been fought because of religion. Men have been murdered and tortured in the name of religion. God himself has been mocked and held up to scorn and ridicule because of religion. Empty form – the organisations and trappings of men, without the empowering of God's life-giving Spirit – is at best mere human effort and at worst demonic. Paul describes these people as 'having a form of godliness but denying its power'. (2 Timothy 3:5). His conclusion is:

> Have nothing to do with them. They are the kind who worm their way into homes and gain control over weak-willed women, who are loaded down with sins and are swayed by all kinds of evil desires, always learning but never able to acknowledge the truth (2 Timothy 3:5–7).

Religion and faith can only exist together when faith in Christ and living in the Spirit of God are the goals. Never make an idol of any kind of religion, whether a particular denomination or a rigid way of doing things. You only have to look at creation to know that the Holy Spirit isn't rigid. We shouldn't have to shoe-horn him into meetings!

Unless you are hearing or have heard from God you are unlikely to be serving him. So before we spend our time on vast and fruitless outreaches let's wait on him, attuned to the voice of his Spirit in our hearts. Then we must obey that voice.

He said to Simon, 'Put out into deep water, and let down the nets for a catch.' Simon answered, 'Master, we've worked hard all night and haven't caught

anything. But because you say so, I will let down the
nets.' When they had done so, they caught such a
large number of fish that their nets began to break
(Luke 5:4–6).

Simon had to call for his partners to bring another
boat. They filled both boats so full of fish that they
began to sink. The point of all this wasn't to teach
Simon about fishing; it was to instruct him about how
to spread the gospel! Jesus says to him and to us, 'Don't
be afraid; from now on you will catch men.'

But how do we do it? By working all night? No. By
adapting business strategies to maket the kingdom?
No. We do it by listening to and obeying the voice of
the one who sees the hearts of men, who knows how to
soften those hearts; the one who knows when people
are ready and where those people are. We are back to
battle plans, strategies. The only way to proceed is to
receive directions from God by waiting on him in
prayer, and then to pray through and carry out those
directions.

The gospel, clear and anointed

So how are you going to present the gospel? The Spirit
will show you the best strategy for the particular
individuals or nation you are praying about.

God's strategy may even mean you don't witness at
all with words. Often, especially where relatives are
concerned, the best way of witnessing is by your
behaviour. But there will come a time when a clear,
anointed presentation of the gospel is vital. If you're
not going to bring it then you need to pray for a
credible witness. Pray that the Lord will raise one up.
God has his people everywhere; God has his secret

agents! Through your prayer a release of the Holy Spirit can take place and someone on a bus or train or somewhere else in the world can not only hear the gospel but the meaning of the gospel can become clear to him.

There are whole systems of theology – fat textbooks that try to explain how people come to Christ. If people are dead in their trespasses and sins then what causes them to live? Do they first get resurrected by their own faith and then receive salvation? Or does Jesus save them and then bring them to life? How does it happen; what's the order? Jesus himself tells us that you cannot analyse the rebirth to that degree:

> Jesus answered, 'I tell you the truth, no-one can enter the kingdom of God unless he is born of water and the Spirit. Flesh gives birth to flesh, but the Spirit gives birth to spirit. You should not be surprised at my saying, You must be born again. The wind blows wherever it pleases. You hear its sound, but you cannot tell where it comes from or where it is going. So it is with everyone born of the Spirit' (John 3:5–8).

While it is true to say that without the help of the Holy Spirit no one can come to God, it is also true that each individual has to make his or her own choice. Everyone has to carry the moral responsibility for their own choices.

Jesus tells us clearly that his death on the cross will release an anointing of the Holy Spirit upon the world, an anointing that will not only bring judgement and conviction of sin but that will also draw the world to himself: 'Now is the time for judgement on this world; now the prince of this world will be driven out. But I, when I am lifted up from the earth, will draw all men to myself' (John 12:31–32).

When Jesus was lifted up on the cross he died for the sins of the entire world. He opened the way for all to come to God. He also released the drawing power of the Holy Spirit so that people might also be able to come to him and accept the life he offers. When we proclaim the gospel in a clear, direct way, having been sent into a situation with the specific words for that situation and that people, then we are lifting up Jesus for individuals and for nations. When he is lifted up the anointing of the Holy Spirit is released. People are freed to make their own decisions. The Holy Spirit can go about his work of convincing and convicting. He can counteract every other negative influence that prevents people from seeing the reality of the choice before them. Everyone can be drawn to Jesus – that's the power of the gospel. But how will they respond to him? That must remain their choice.

Pulling down strongholds

I've already mentioned how the enemy has blinded the minds of unbelievers so that they cannot perceive or understand the truth of the gospel (2 Corinthians 4:4). And we've already seen that we can work together with the Spirit of God in opposing and driving him out. Once he had every right to dominate us but now he is here under false pretences, as it were, trying to hide from us his vulnerability to the authority of Christ. He is quite an expert at doing it too, using every accusation, lie and deception drawn from a very large arsenal. Don't ever underestimate him; he would make a marvellous prosecutor!

We are talking here about powerful fallen beings but

beings who, despite their cunning and their hatred, have been beaten and humiliated by Jesus and must submit to him. In the name of Jesus we can use our delegated authority to bind the strong man. When we are living in the vine he has no more authority over us than he can deceive us into believing he has.

That may be fine for us but what about the world? What about those whom the enemy is still able to dominate; those who may hardly recognise him let alone know how to defeat him? Scripture tells us that behind human government, politics and historical events, lie the influences of demonic forces. How can we combat these?

> For though we live in the world, we do not wage war as the world does. The weapons we fight with are not the weapons of the world. On the contrary, they have divine power to demolish strongholds. We demolish arguments and every pretension that sets itself up against the knowledge of God and we take captive every thought to make it obedient to Christ (2 Corinthians 10:3–5).

This passage of Scripture shows that strongholds largely exist in false and pretentious beliefs. I have a stronghold and so do you: our stronghold is the Lord! A thought life that is submitted to Christ is a marvellous thing because it reflects the character of God. It can be creative and honest, open or full of hidden truths. It can be sensitive, wonderfully subtle, or strong and colourful; of breathtaking intelligence or piercing simplicity; playful or sober. And it is wholesome, full of life, love and justice. Never proud, vain or self-seeking. In fact, we are probably unable to fully describe the capabilities of a human mind submitted to God because through the Holy Spirit those possibilities

are endless. Let's use our biblical mindset, our Godly
stronghold, and through it dare to demolish every
argument and pretension that sets itself up against the
knowledge of God.

I'm sure you don't need me to tell you how pretentious imaginations hook people into following ideas –
and not only following: people sacrifice their lives on
the altar of vain and foolish speculations as well as down-
right lies served up as truth. When these pretentious
imaginations are in places of authority, many people
are ensnared or destroyed. But don't be fooled into
thinking these strongholds are vainglorious things that
are easy to debunk; it isn't simply a matter of verbally
pricking someone's bubble. A stronghold is just that –
strong. We are talking about hard and militant mind-
sets, often forged through generations of understandable but misdirected outrage, anger and bitterness.

Strongholds of sin

How do we go about demolishing these strongholds?
Not by having a Scripture-slanging match! Not by
accusing and condemning people; who accuses and
condemns? A stronghold is not just a few demons you
can elbow out before lunchtime. It is a spiritual structure that has a powerful hold over a situation, a nation
or a group of people. It can even be related to
particular geographical areas.

Scripture gives us enough evidence to suggest that as
historical events take place and sin operates through
human agents on the earth, the enemy finds his opportunity to enter in and begin establishing his rule. If
there was no sin he would have no hold on anything,
so where we have situations of historical sin and the
repetition of that, we find the enemy increasingly

manifesting his presence in and through humanity. The human side of this manifestation can be found in social problems or particular moral problems of an area.

When we find out how the enemy has sown his seeds, how the root of that stronghold has developed and what its fruit is then we shall know how to attack it at its foundations and destroy it. But more about this in the next chapter.

You can use observation, historical research and the discerning of spirits to pinpoint targets accurately. Your church in your location can take the sword of the Spirit, God's Word, into specific and real situations – the truth that is able to pierce 'even to the division of soul and spirit, and of joints and marrow'.

Your church can pray! We can all intercede, we can cry out to God for insight, for strategies to undo the harm, to cut through the enemy's snares. Don't do this on your own; meet an army with an army. Beseech the Lord to raise up people to take their stand in the front line, people who have submitted their hearts and their imaginations to their creator, people whom Jesus himself will choose and release to fly high, free and strong!

We must pray for a great preparing of hearts, for the Holy Spirit to do his work, to bring his anointing to the Church and to the world. We must know and use our authority in Christ, our authority to bring down every stronghold and deal with every wicked spirit that has been assigned to keep people in blindness. Bind on earth those things already bound in heaven and loose on earth those things already loosed in heaven. Pray! Pray and bring down the false beliefs, the prejudices and the stumbling-blocks. And when we are called, let's be ready to go boldly as ministers of the gospel and say to the enemy 'The game's up, get out!'

A few years ago we were challenged as a church by the nation of Benin. A tiny West African republic situated on the borders of Ghana, Nigeria and Togo, Benin has been held for generations in the grip of satanic darkness. It is the birth place of Voodoo which has put up stiff and hostile resistance to evangelism despite many years of missionary activity. We felt very strongly that the Lord wanted us to get alongside the national Christians and help them break through with the gospel, especially in the unevangelised rural areas dominated by Voodoo powers.

Conscious of the spiritual battles ahead we set about seeking God and his strategies. We knew mere evangelism was not enough; it was also important to encourage new converts to group into churches under local leadership. So we drew up plans for an extensive training programme. I led a small team on a reconnaissance mission into Benin. The purpose was to spy out the land and assess the strength of spiritual opposition. It was severe, but we began to pray. Once more I felt the reality of Paul's words: 'We wrestle against principalities and powers, against the rulers of the darkness of this age, against the spiritual hosts of wickedness in the heavenly places' (Ephesians 6:12 NKJV).

Though the struggle was intense we prayed on until we sensed a significant release in the spiritual realm. It was as if something gave way in the heavenlies. Since that time we have sent many teams into Benin with the double strategy of intercession and evangelism. Many hundreds of people have been won for Christ and scores of new churches established right in the very worst centres of Voodoo.

Spiritual warfare is real, and prayer and evangelism are its chief weapons. The same principles we have proved in Africa and other developing nations work in the western world as well. We have our spiritual strongholds too. They may not be the open demonism of Voodoo, though occultism and paganism are rising once more in the West. The demonic influences may not be operating so much in our society through literal idols of wood or stone. But they can be traced in the false philosophies of humanism, atheism and materialism and manifest in our rejection of God and his standards for our lives. We must avoid the paternalistic attitude of some Western Christians who accept open spiritual warfare as necessary in Africa and Asia, but are blind to the satanic struggles taking place on our doorstep.

Praying the promises of God

'Again I tell you if two of you on earth agree about anything you ask for it will be done for you by my Father in heaven. For where two or three come together in my name, there I am with them' (Matthew 18:19–20).

Statistics have shown that the majority of people who have come to Christ in large-scale evangelistic meetings are brought along and prayed for by people as for example in the prayer triplet system.

A prayer triplet is three people who regularly meet to pray for three people each who don't yet know the Lord. Then they invite them to an event where they are going to hear the gospel preached. When three people agree and intercede together like this, believing God with each other and waiting on him for instructions, powerful things happen.

In the run-up to Billy Graham's 'Mission '89', many of the prayer triplets organised by the participating churches reported those on their prayer lists coming to Christ even before the mission began. One programme we have recently adopted in our church is called 'Group, Gather and Grow', and it encourages people to pray for and to reach out to their non-Christian friends and personal contacts. We are finding targeted prayer in the context of evangelism to be a powerful combination which is bringing new life to many hundreds of people.

One of our groups was led by a fairly recent convert from the martial arts. The Holy Spirit gave the group special sensitivity to the needs of people still held in the grip of the false religious beliefs often attached to these practices. They found many people involved in the martial arts were searching for spiritual truth. In prayer the group developed a particular awareness of those who were ready to listen and respond to the Christian message. As a result they were able to concentrate their evangelistic efforts on those most open to accept the gospel.

Take God at his word. Meeting in triplets provides balance and extra strength. 'Though one may be over-powered, two can defend themselves. A cord of three strands is not quickly broken' (Ecclesiastes 4:12). When three ask in the agreement of the Spirit, they shall be given whatever they ask! Praying this way is acting on the promises of God.

Do you know that God saves families? In many places in the world where there is strong family solidarity it is not unusual for whole families to come to Christ or whole tribes, even. There are many promises in Scripture relating to households that you can pray into being. For instance, the Israelites were told by God to select a lamb for every household (Exodus 12–13). It was their Passover lamb, the blood of which would save them from destruction. This is a picture for us too. You can say, 'Lord Jesus, you're the Lamb of God and it says "A lamb for a house." This is my house and your blood was shed as a lamb for this household.' We can claim this truth and establish it in prayer.

Peter tells the crowds (Acts 2:38–39) that if they repent and are baptised in the name of Jesus they will receive the Holy Spirit. This promise, he says, is not only for them but for their children too. Then there is the jailer who fell down trembling at the feet of Paul and Silas (Acts 16:27–34). He asked what he should do to be saved. They told him that if he believed in the Lord Jesus then he and his household would be saved. The outcome? The whole family believed and was baptised!

Paul speaks about relationships within the family and how one believing partner sanctifies the unbelieving partner. The children of such unions, Paul tells us, are 'holy' (1 Corinthians 7:14). This doesn't mean that members of a family are automatically saved by one person's faith but it does mean that they are in a good place to come to faith in Christ: they are intimately involved with someone who has access to the throne of God.

What about the promises for the nations? 'Ask of me and I will make the nations your inheritance, the ends of the earth your possession' (Psalm 2:8). There are really no limits on what the Spirit of God wants to achieve in and through you and me, the Church, the bride of Christ. Start where you are. Pray and release his anointing; then follow wherever he leads you.

Breaking through

Praying in the promises of God involves us working with the Holy Spirit to bring about a breakthrough. This is a task that is given to us to do. Angels are not sent to preach the gospel; it's not their job. Jesus is not going to preach the gospel anymore, except through us. Miraculous things may happen but they don't happen out of the blue from the hand of an arbitrary God; they happen when we pray – even if we're on the other side of the world. We must wake up to our great calling in Christ! 'Now to him who is able to do exceeding abundantly above all that we ask or think, according to the power that works in us' (Ephesians 3:20). The greatest breakthrough of all time was when Jesus passed through the heavens and became our advocate before the Father. As a result, God's ability and power is made available for us and it works in us. God does not have to give us a new breakthrough – the one he has already achieved is enough! He does not expect us to break through for ourselves. He is, however, going to eable us to lay hold of the breakthrough he has accomplished. We can break through in prayer, by his power!

Stepping into the victory that Jesus has already won and administering that victory is going to involve us in warfare. The account of David's battle against the Philistines in 2 Samuel 5:17–25, clearly shows that God is the God of the Breakthrough. Let's look closely at what happened there. Note how David carried out the Lord's instructions.

David has not long been anointed King over Israel. When the Philistines hear about it they react immediately against his anointing and the authority that he has. They mobilise their entire army to search for him.

News that they are on the way reaches David so he goes down to Israel's stronghold. The Philistines have spread themselves out in the Valley of Rephaim. David asks God what he should do.

'Shall I go and attack the Philistines? Will you hand them over to me?'

'Go, for I will surely hand the Philistines over to you,' answers the Lord.

David attacks and defeats his enemies.

'As waters break out,' he says, 'the Lord has broken

out against my enemies before me.' In the parallel passage (1 Chronicles 14:11), David adds 'by my hand' showing that God uses human beings to assert on the earth his purposes that are accomplished in heaven. The battle ground was named 'Baal Perazim' which means 'The Lord breaks out' (or breaks through).

David and his men disposed of the idols which the Philistines had abandoned when they were forced to flee. Here is the real issue: the question was a spiritual one – who is the true and living God? This single question is also the theme of the whole story of mankind. History is moving towards its climax when Jesus Christ will return and put down all opposing rule and authority, including every force of false religion.

This, however, was not the end of the story. The enemy didn't give up easily. We see the Philistines regrouping in the same valley.

David goes again to the Lord and asks what he should do. This time the strategy is different.

'Do not go straight up,' answers the Lord, 'but circle round behind them and attack them in front of the balsam trees. As soon as you hear the sound of marching in the tops of the balsam trees, move quickly, because that will mean the Lord has gone out in front of you to strike the Philistine army.'

David did as the Lord commanded and he struck down the Philistines all the way from Gibeon to Gezer.

The Philistines had reacted against David's anointing. What was David's response? He strengthened himself in the stronghold and so must we – in our stronghold, the Lord. 'The Lord is my rock, my fortress and my deliverer; my God is my rock, in whom I take refuge. He is my shield and the horn of my salvation, my stronghold' (Psalms 18:2).

What did David do? He enquired of the Lord. And so must we. Being led by the Holy Spirit is crucial at all

times, especially at war. David defeated his enemy; i
was something that God enabled David himself to do
David prayed; the Lord gave him the strategy; he acted
on instructions; he was victorious.

Look again. Have you noticed how persistent the
enemy is? The Philistines re-group and return. Does
David act in presumption and charge off to attack
them? No. What does he do? He goes back to the Lord
who sees men's hearts, who knows everyone's battle
plan.

This time the strategy is different. David is to wait.
The Lord will go out before him and act on his behalf.
David is to follow. Again, David prayed; the Lord gave
him the strategy; he acted on instructions; he was
victorious. This is how we receive our breakthrough!

11 Creative Prayer Strategy

Firm foundations

Our Father in heaven, hallowed be your name, your kingdom come, your will be done on earth as it is in heaven (Matthew 6:9–10).

When the disciples asked Jesus to teach them to pray, he gave them a prayer pattern – a framework, if you like. In the verses I have just quoted, Jesus is encouraging us to remember that our Father is in heaven, that he is on the throne and in control; we can know the reality of his greatness and presence with us. We are to recognise his glory and holiness; we can pray that it be manifested and received in specific ways.

Jesus wants us to pray for his Father's rule to be extended, both in our own lives as we increasingly submit to his reign, and in the lives of others. As we pray, the Holy Spirit will show us specific ways in which they can be accomplished.

The coming of God's kingdom means that the conditions of heaven are manifested on earth. This will not take place fully until Jesus returns but, in the meantime, we are to pray for God's revealed will to be done in specific situations on earth.

Creative prayer is about the creator establishing his plans in our hearts; we in prayer and faith lay hold of them, then follow them through: we co-operate with the Holy Spirit in bringing them into being on the earth. It always sounds much more complicated when you describe it than it actually feels in practice.

Any group of people wanting to move out into these things must have a secure basis from which to start. The Lord led us at KT to first undergird the church, otherwise it would have been like trying to reach out with no foundation. As that wonderful hymn states so clearly: 'The Church's one foundation is Jesus Christ, her Lord.'

This is where we began: with repentance, admitting our earlier mistakes of letting our busy ministries crowd out the priority of personal and corporate prayer. We had to come once again and establish Jesus, and only Jesus, at the heart of our lives and our church.

Then we took the prayer line I have already mentioned: 'My house will be called a house of prayer for all nations' (Mark 11:17). We had been called to restore God's house, to make it once again a house of prayer. When it had become a house of prayer then everything else would follow.

It was about this time that we began to implement a new prayer strategy. I don't mean to imply here that we simply had to pray more; I'm talking about a new earnestness, a new quality of prayer that the Holy Spirit wanted to move us into. We called this prayer initiative the 'watchman' programme after Jesus' question to the disciples at Gethsemane, 'Could you not keep watch for one hour?' (Mark 14:37).

The task was first to build up the walls of prayer and intercession in the church. Our strategy was rooted in Jesus' question. We did not want to let him down. It is so easy for a people to give way to a spirit of slumber, complacency and comfort. When we do that the enemy has us just where he wants us. We become ineffective, useless or worse – actually destructive to the kingdom of God.

The watchman programme was never imposed as a formula; we didn't want it to become rigid and rule-bound; the Lord wants willing workers. The idea is that anyone who wants to be involved spends one specific hour a week in prayer. There are five minutes to get freshened up before the Lord. Then ten minutes to pray for the other watchmen: for their protection; for the outpouring of God's grace on their personal lives; that their own needs will be met as they watch in prayer for others; that the whole programme will be kept alive and fresh by the Holy Spirit.

Then fifteen minutes is spent praying for families in the church, building up their walls. Fifteen minutes is for the church itself, and the final fifteen minutes is spent praying for the city.

It is a guide to show people how to pray for an hour. It is mostly followed, though it doesn't really matter if someone spends thirty minutes praying for families or even a whole hour praying for the city. Soon the hours were organised so that there were over one thousand people praying round the clock. Later we developed an intensive one-hour-a-day programme with over two hundred people participating. We had constant twenty-four-hour prayer cover – a powerful basis from which to move out!

Prayer-soaking

We began to soak everything we did in powerful prayer. The watchmen were providing twenty-four-hour cover, and the Wednesday 'spearhead' meeting was providing the inspiration and the prayer agenda for smaller groups and individuals to pray through during the week. In addition to this, prayer partners and prayer triplets were meeting to seek God for various intermittent needs circulated to them in a monthly prayer letter.

Then we turned our attention to Sundays. A group of people began to gather before the main Sunday meeting to pray for God's anointing and to pray through anything that the Spirit might bring to them. The first two rows of seats in the meeting itself, occupied mainly by the pastoral staff, became intercession seats. Now anyone sitting in them and other specially designated places in the building, spends time in covering prayer while the main meeting is actually in progress. In addition to this there is another group of people in a room at the back of the church praying for the technicians, the musicians, the congregation, the speaker, in fact anyone involved at all with that meeting. And they are available should any direct warfare prayer be needed.

All our meetings usually include a time of preaching and ministry to people with specific needs. All this is supported by prayer teams who assemble in a different room and spend the time in worship, covering prayer and intercession. The Friday meeting usually finishes at about ten thirty when, if it is the last Friday of the month, people start arriving for one of the many all-night prayer meetings which kick off at about eleven and generally finish at six the following morning. And then there are all the various departmental prayer meetings.

You can see that it takes a praying church to do this. No one could possibly do it all. Yet the result of us all accepting our priestly function alongside Jesus, our high priest, is power in the heavenly realms, protection in the earthly ones, victory and breakthrough in many areas, phenomenal growth and the companionship and the blessing of the Holy Spirit. When we show our God that we really mean business he will answer our cry; he will pour out his grace; he will enable and empower us.

Repentance, authority and strategy

It is futile to have a marvellous prayer strategy if we don't have the authority to carry it out. It will just be so much energy dissipated; an ineffective and discouraging waste of everyone's times. We can't take authority over an enemy who has ground in us to begin with.

I have mentioned in a previous chapter how, in 1989, we were given this strong prayer line which we meditated on and prayed over for several years: 'No longer will violence be heard in your land, nor ruin or destruction within your borders, but you will call your walls salvation and your gates praise' (Isaiah 60:18).

The enemy comes to ruin and destroy but Christ comes to bring life. The ruining, in our area particularly but elsewhere as well, is the ruining of lives by drug addiction, prostitution, sexual bondage, exploitation, domestic violence, marital stress, divorce, separation and the tearing up of families. People can be destroyed from the inside out because of sin, and behind that is a wicked spirit of destruction and a spirit of murder and violence.

Yet, in that verse, God had promised us deliverance from all of that. As we began to think and pray on these things the Lord led us to focus on three main obstacles to the gospel in our area. And not only in our area, but also in ourselves!

The first was the slave trade. The suffering and anguish that this caused still affects us today, manifesting in racial tensions, violence and discrimination. There are two sides to this issue.

The slave trade was largely European exploitation: a cruel and vile trafficking in human life. We are still reaping the bitter fruits of it. God is not going to bless a nation whose economic foundations were built on bondage and blood money, not until there is real repentance. There needs to be a great deal of repentance in our nation because of its sinful past. God is just, and he doesn't ignore sin:

'See I am going to rouse them out of the places to which you sold them and I will return on your own heads what you have done' (Joel 3:7).

On the other hand, it was not only white people who exploited Africans in the slave trade. One African tribe would often sell another into slavery and the fruits of that are being seen today in tribal conflicts. These are behind so much of the political, social and economic difficulty in Africa today. Wherever there's been hurt the human reaction is usually one of rebellion, hatred and unforgiveness, which is the biggest bondage of them all. I believe that many black people today need to reject that legacy of bitterness in their hearts.

The second area that we were led to look as was the destruction brought about by drugs and the things that go with them: theft, violence and criminal activities of all kinds. This can be traced back to the opium trade with China, and Britain is still a major centre for drug trafficking. 'Such is the end of all who go after ill gotten gain, it takes away the lives of those who get it' (Proverbs 1:19).

The third thing we need to concern ourselves with was the whole are of greed. This island nation has a history of greed and piracy on the high seas that has just moved location. Today it manifests in dishonesty, fraud, insider-dealing, avarice; in short, worship of the god of money.

We had to search our hearts and make our own confessions. We asked God to cleanse and to forgive us. Only then could we truly begin to align ourselves with his righteous purposes.

Scripture tells us that we have all sinned, that we have all fallen short of the glory of God. Righteousness exalts a nation but sin is a reproach to any people. If we are to deal with the fruit of sin in our nation or our city we first have to deal with it in our own hearts and lives. We need to ask the Lord for a deep and powerful cleansing. The blood of Jesus avails for the peoples of Africa, the West Indies and Europe, down through the centuries, for successive generations who have been eating the fruit of this bitter root of sin. We asked God to come and lay his axe to the root, to remove all hurt and bitterness and anger from us, all arrogance, all prejudice, all discrimination and then to bring his healing.

The power of repentance

One important lesson we learned was to bring the sins of the nation to the Lord. The Bible teaches both individual and corporate responsibility for sins. We are personally guilty for our own sins, but we cannot completely disassociate ourselves from the sins of our nation. Both the present and past sins of a nation affect those in that nation. We are all part of our sinful environment, often being deeply influenced and bound up in it all. This, together with the intercessory principle of identification I have already covered in Chapter 7 means that we will sometimes be deeply conscious of the sins of the nation and how they affect us as individuals.

Under such conviction it will be necessary to confess

both national and personal sins before the Lord and ask him to forgive them. The prophet Daniel did that when he was interceding for the people of God in exile. It was time for the prophetic word of restoration given seventy years before through Jeremiah to be fulfilled. In a most personal and heartfelt way Daniel earnestly confessed the sins of Judah:

> I prayed to the LORD my God and confessed: 'O Lord, the great and awesome God, who keeps his covenant of love with all who love him and obey his commands, we have sinned and done wrong. We have been wicked and have rebelled; we have turned away from your commands and laws' (Daniel 9:4–5).

At the end of this passionate prayer, Daniel cries out to God for his forgiveness to come to the nation: 'O Lord, listen! O Lord, forgive! O Lord, hear and act! For your sake, O my God, do not delay, because your city and your people bear your Name' (Daniel 9:19).

While we can confess the sins of others, it is important to understand that we cannot personally repent of those sins. The idea of surrogate repentance, repenting for someone else's sin is unbiblical. However, we can repent of our part in the sin: how it affects us, our reactions, struggles and blindness; our complicity, conscious or unconscious. The way sin affects individuals, families and whole nations is extremely subtle and complex. How can it be humanly possible to trace sin's deceitful course in our own lives let alone see its hidden operation in the social political and economic history of our nation? Only God can see sin as it really is and how it works like yeast throughout the whole of society. As a polluted water supply causes disease to spread to all who drink it, our society nurtures sin and we don't always know we are being infected.

Take the abortion issue, for example. How far would we recognise our part in the mass murder of millions of unborn children? We may never have condoned to participated in an abortion, but what have we done to persuade, protest and pray about this blot on our national conscience? Have we helped in a practical way those who socially or psychologically think that abortion is the only way out for them? Have we stood on the other side of the road and criticised or perhaps just buried our head in the sand? Have we really done all that we could to protest and bring about change when it comes to this issue alone? Or, to take another example, what about our part in the unrighteous economy of our nation? How have we contributed to the state of our national economy? Have we done our best at work? Have we been content to sponge of state benefit when we really did have a choice? What about the basis of modern Western wealth? Didn't much of it come from unrighteous trade, exploitation and the plunder of other nations? As we live off the fruit of these economic roots we are sharing in national sin. We need to repent and ask God to take away the deeply ingrained sin and guilt of our nations.

But for God's forgiveness to flow to any nation, that nation must turn to the Lord. Repentance must begin with the Church, its leaders and people. Then the nation's leaders and the ordinary people of the land must acknowledge God's power and righteousness. This is one more reason why intercession and evangelism must go hand in hand. We need both hands of prayer *and* evangelism to take hold of a nation's problems. Evangelism brings the call to turn to Christ and find forgiveness and intercession creates the spiritual environment that makes it happen.

Having dealt with these things at a level of depth in

our own lives we were free to take authority in prayer over these obstacles wherever we found them rearing up and threatening to dominate situations. In the same way, your church can look at the spiritual roots of problems in your local area or your nation as a whole. Then in a spirit of humility and repentance you can call on the Lord to break these spiritual bondages and bring a powerful release to the gospel through evangelism calling people back to God.

Prayer strategy in relation to a specific event

Carnivals began as times of rejoicing over sins forgiven; they were church celebrations of Christ's victory. The Notting Hill carnival is believed to be the biggest in Europe and had, for many years, a reputation about as far removed from the original meaning as you can get. Even if you're not of a nervous disposition you used to worry when, every August, you found yourself surrounded by murders, violence, drug-related crime, riot police and the penetrating searchlights of helicopters thudding overhead.

At KT we felt this event had been hijacked by the enemy. It was time to begin taking it back.

The first time we met specifically to pray for the Carnival was during the eighties. We spent whole nights in prayer. First we prepared ourselves, examining our own consciences and confessing anything we needed to confess. We looked at scriptures relevant to the situation. And in the name of Jesus we came against the enemy.

Now, every January we pray into the planning of the Carnival and we reserve a whole night to pray over that. In the space of a night you can get a breakthrough.

At other times, too, we come together and seek God to move upon it.

With the great strength, faith and confidence that comes from the fact that we were thoroughly prepared by the Holy Spirit, we began to arise against the spirit of violence and destruction. Corporately, we took authority. Together we spoke out God's promises to us (Isaiah 60:18). Some of us were building up the walls of salvation, others were tearing down the walls of violence, ruin and destruction. And as we bound the enemy we began to loose, in the name of Jesus, salvation and praise. We stood in the gap, entering into the spiritual realm over the situation, and we used our authority in Jesus' name. We prayed against lawlessness and we prayed positively for that to be replaced by respect for the law; in prayer, racial unrest was replaced by reconciliation; gang warfare fell to community spirit; gratuitous violence was replaced with love for one's neighbour; destruction was bound and restoration loosed; looting and greed were replaced by unselfishness.

This may seem strange to those who have never prayed like this but you will find that as we pray for and manifest the spirit of the positive ourselves, the negative is driven out. What was the immediate result? There was a sudden drop in arrests.

About two years after we had started to pray for the Carnival a local policeman came to the church. One of the members who had been involved in organising the intercession told him how we had been supporting the police in prayer, asking that they would be given wisdom and restraint, especially around the time of the Carnival. The policeman was astounded.

'Now I know what happened,' he said.

'What do you mean?' the member asked.

'We couldn't understand why there were no riots

when we arrested people,' he explained. 'It was almost nerve-racking, waiting for the explosions that never happened.'

We can't sit back and say that August is a peaceful month yet; there's more to do. There are still occasional stabbings and the accident and emergency unit at St Giles Hospital will tell you that this is still a tough time, but the Carnival itself has, for several years now, been a spectacle to truly enjoy.

Implementing Christ's victory

Jesus Christ is Lord.

> God exalted him to the highest place and gave him the name that is above every name, that at the name of Jesus every knee should bow, in heaven and on earth and under the earth and every tongue confess that Jesus Christ is Lord, to the glory of God the Father (Philippians 2:9–11).

Every tongue shall confess the Lordship of Christ, even the tongues of his enemies. We must begin to work, to move and to minister from that position of authority. There are many ways in which we can do this together; all sorts of exciting and dynamic prayer events are possible, taking prayer out of the walls of a church building.

Breaking out

The first major prayer event that we held together as a church could loosely be called a 'prayer drive', though there were almost as many involved in prayer at the central church as there were out in coaches and cars. The most important thing to remember about a prayer event is that it is hard work in the Spirit; we are there to do business on God's behalf. We are not out in our civilian clothes, seeing the sights with a bit of prayer thrown in. God doesn't want religious tourists; he wants a working and operational spiritual army.

The idea for the planning of a prayer drive began when several people indpendently had the idea – the overriding picture was that of a structure like a wheel with spokes. Other spokes were criss-crossing it, providing strength and support.

Then, in a meeting, these pictures were confirmed and further explained by a prophetic word from the Lord. Our strategy was to dice up the area of London, drawing the lines where we felt God wanted us to go. We were to begin 'spiritual mapping'.

We did some initial research, driving around the North and South circular roads, London's orbital roads, gathering information and noting down places of interest. Patterns became evident, things began to occur to us; the Spirit began to direct our hearts and minds.

We broke the information into sections; each section with some very definite places to bring before God's throne. A taxi driver who attended the church worked out routes.

On the day of the drive the church met together in the main building at six forty-five. The first thing we did was to get out of our civilian clothes and put on our military ones; this drive was not just a physical act, it was going to be a spiritual one.

The effect of anything we seek to do here in the physical is won or lost first of all by battle in the heavenlies. Without the full armour of God you cannot take your stand against the devil's schemes. You will move forward, you will have a degree of success but there will be a comeback in your own life. God has given us this armour – it is so important that we don't go naked into battle!

We spent time reminding ourselves of these things and claiming afresh our right to intercede as priestly warriors. Then we worshipped God together. Between five and six hundred willing troops were assembled, all ready to do business, praying for God's anointing in the unity of the Spirit and in alignment with the will of God for the city.

By eight-thirty that evening six coaches had started on their routes, fifty committed intercessors on each. In addition we sent four crack-shot (sort of spiritual SAS) teams in small, unmarked cars to spiritually strategic places.

I was linked with the travelling teams by ten radio telephones and we broadcast my conversations with each group over the PA system to the rest of the church. Our job was to pray, worship and intercede alongside the teams.

During that evening we learned a great deal. The people in the coaches found they were more sensitive to spiritual atmosphere, discerning strongholds in the Spirit as they passed through different districts, praying together as the Spirit led. Back at the church we flowed from prayer and praise into binding and loosing and then began to intercede on behalf of specific areas, sometimes with tears, travail and confession. We began to identify with the sin of the city; enough sin to deserve God's wrath. We started to stand in the gap. Words of knowledge and prophecy came together to give us a deeper understanding of our spiritual map and a greater realisation of the importance of our prayers.

Yes, we do deserve judgement, but God's grace is greater still. His desire is to pour it out but that is conditional not inevitable. The first condition is that the people of God line up with his purposes and begin to intercede, to pray for the Spirit of God to be released over the city. All this is hard work but when you're dressed in your armour you don't go out on parade! You pray in the Spirit on all occasions with the right kind of prayer for the situation, the right keys for the right locks.

Since then, prayer walks, prayer marches and many other forms of creative praying have become the norm for us. We go to places of strategic historical and spiritual importance and, as the Holy Spirit leads us, we break spiritual bondages linked to these sites and pray for a release of God's grace and power. Another large-scale prayer event, similar to the prayer drive, was the Thames prayer cruise. This time we took over several tourist boats and cruised up and down the Thames praying about the issues suggested by the many historical and strategic landmarks found along the banks of the Thames river. It was amazing to see how many places of national financial, political and religious significance we found there. The prayer, praise and general excitement of the event certainly made an impression on the captains and their crew. I don't think they had seen anything quite like it!

All these prayer efforts, along with those of many other churches, including many united prayer events are changing the spiritual face of our city. This is demonstrated by the rapidly increasing rate of church growth in London. Certainly in my experience, it seems that from the moment we pushed forward this new prayer emphasis in the early 1990s we saw break-through after breakthrough. Now people are coming to Christ daily. There is an increase in healings and signs and wonders. People are experiencing a deeper work of God in their lives. The spiritual climate has changed.

Supercharging prayer

God always looks upon the heart. If we are not serious about our dealings with him why should he answer us? It is this earnestness, this seriousness, that the Lord looks for and responds to.

There are several ways we can show God we mean business, that our prayers are not idle words but an expression of our hearts. Scripture is littered with examples of the Lord responding to generosity of heart, sacrificial giving, vows and memorial offerings.

Remember Hannah and the turmoil of heart she experienced? Provoked for years by her rival because of her childlessness she sought the Lord 'in bitterness of soul' (1 Samuel 1:10), praying and weeping.

> O LORD Almighty, if you will only look upon your servant's misery and remember me, and not forget your servant but give her a son, then I will give him to the LORD for all the days of his life, and no razor will ever be used on his head (1 Samuel 1:11).

Hannah was so distraught that Eli the High Priest accused her of being drunk (just to add to her troubles!). She made a solemn vow to God that if he gave her a son she would give the child back to him. This was a sacrificial offering indeed.

As soon as the boy was weaned Hannah took him to the temple and gave him into Eli's keeping. What a hard thing to do! But God blessed her. Eli prayed to the Lord asking him to give her more children. She subsequently had three sons and two daughters!

What did God do for Cornelius, the Roman centurion who was a generous and godly man, a man of prayer? An angel appeared to him in a vision saying:

'Your prayers and gifts to the poor have come up as a memorial offering before God' (Acts 10:4). This man was known and loved by God. For his sake the Lord spoke to Peter, changing the disciple's attitude towards Gentiles and Gentile customs. The Lord made sure that Cornelius heard the gospel, then saved his whole household and filled them all with the Holy Spirit. We have a God who sees and judges the hidden thoughts of our hearts. You cannot buy God's blessing, but faithfulness and generosity of spirit will not be forgotten.

Giving, whether it be financial help for the poor or giving our time to others and to God in prayer, means that we are known in the heavenly realms; we are heard and we shall receive. 'Give and it will be given to you. A good measure, pressed down, shaken together and running over, will be poured into your lap. For with the measure you use, it will be measured to you' (Luke 6:38).

Of course, the most familiar and one of the most neglected way of supercharging our prayer is by fasting, which we're going to consider next.

The value and power of fasting

Fasting is the voluntary abstinence of good and/or drink for spiritual purposes and is closely related to prayer and intercession. The whole purpose of it is to seek God. It is a sign of the seriousness of a situation and is for the times when we need to get to grips with God in a deeply solemn way. By fasting, it is as if we are saying to God, 'Lord, this situation that has brought me to my knees before you is of greater concern to me than my normal bodily needs of food and drink.'

We are talking here about single-mindedness; putting aside our normal routine and giving that time wholly to the Lord, concentrating on interceding for needs which are of vital importance.

Isaiah chapter 58 makes it clear that it is not physical bonds that are broken through fasting but spiritual ones. A fast should reflect our seriousness about marching forward to establish truth, righteousness and justice. It's no good us just going without food – what does this profit ourselves or God?

> Is not this the kind of fasting I have chosen: To loose the chains of injustice and untie the cords of the yoke, to set the oppressed free and break every yoke? Is it not to share your food with the hungry and to provide the poor wanderer with shelter – when you see the naked to clothe him, and not to turn away from your own flesh and blood? Then your light will break forth like the dawn and your healing will quickly appear; then your righteousness will go before you and the glory of the LORD will be your rearguard. Then you will call and the LORD will answer; you will cry for help and he will say: Here am I (Isaiah 58:6–9).

One of the problems with fasting, seen so clearly in Old Testament times, is that it can be done in the wrong spirit, either as empty ritual or to impress men or even manipulatively, as a kind of hunger strike to get what you want out of God. Fasting of this nature only makes you weak and irritable; it certainly doesn't impress the Lord!

Much fasting was done for the wrong reasons although there are outstanding examples when nations, cities and individuals turned to the Lord in fasting and God hears and responded to their cries.

Jesus expected his followers to fast and refers to it as though it's taken for granted that they will. For example: 'When you fast' (Matthew 6:16–18); 'they will fast in those days' (Luke 5:35). In the latter quote Jesus is speaking of the time when he would no longer be with his disciples; this, he says, would be a time for fasting. Jesus is no longer physically present among us; this is the time when it is appropriate to fast in order to see God's purposes fulfilled.

Virtually no decision concerning the leadership and direction of the early church was made without fasting. There was fasting for the appointment of elders, the release of ministry and waiting on God for specific direction. It is time for us to restore this discipline to its rightful place in our lives, individually and corporately.

Our bodies are temples of the Holy Spirit and food is God's good gift to us. We need to eat it and we shouldn't abuse our bodies. When we fast it must be because God has called us to it. The call to fast comes as a deep God-given desire to seek the Lord. Sometimes the Spirit will prompt suddenly and other times the desire comes out of responding to a situation or a need known to you.

If you commit yourself to fast as a regular discipline on certain days or at regular intervals you will need to make sure that the Lord is directing you, otherwise the fasting will become nothing more than an external ritualistic practice.

It might be helpful just to mention at this stage what a fast is not. It is not asceticism. Rigorous and unnatural self-denial is an unbiblical practice that harms and dishonours our body, the Lord's Temple. If in doubt take proper medical advice.

Fasting is not self-mortification; it has no value at all as a means of changing our sinful selves and it does not make us holy. It is not wrong to fast over some aspect of sin in our lives but it is repentance and the consecration of the Spirit that changes us, not the fasting.

Fasting has nothing to do with self-merit or self-aggrandisement. If you try to become a spiritual show-off you will receive no reward.

Fasting is an expression of seriousness with God or of grief, mourning and sorrow for sin. Through its practice many things can be achieved for God. It is something we all need to have within our experience. Here are some of its effects: God's presence is manifested, our relationship with the Lord is deepened, authority is given, power is experienced, spiritual sensitivity is heightened, revelation is communicated, satanic opposition is overcome and victory is imparted.

On a purely practical note it is wise to begin with partial fasts – missing a meal, perhaps, or try shorter fasts of one or two days.

Do not go without fluids. Headaches often occur in the early stages. These are due to carbohydrate and caffeine withdrawal. You may find you need to reduce your intake gradually prior to the fast. Be sensitive to the Holy Spirit and fast as he directs. Remember the whole purpose is to seek the Lord. We don't want to do anything that would distract us from this – on the contrary.

Fasting is a much neglected discipline that brings a greater manifestation of spiritual power and anointing, especially with spiritual gifts, that can result in many a breakthrough. Can we really afford to be without it?

Long-term planning

To mature and expand we must have the strategies of the Holy Spirit. We need God's insight and revelation and we have to be willing to wait on him and seek him for it.

Not long after the watchmen were in place, ten major

church strategies for upbuilding and expansion were agreed upon by the leadership at KT. These were in the areas of vision, the power of God, faith, prophetic revelation, prayer and praise, the release of ministries, research and strategy, structure, finance, evangelism and church planting. These initiatives also became the prayer agenda for the watchmen who are still using them as a guide when they come to pray for the church. In this way prayer is woven into the fabric of the church's vision and strategy.

I was thinking a lot about the goals we had set to reach the city. We had wanted to saturate the area with churches, to build something significant. Our projections at the time were that we would plant two hundred churches by the end of the decade.

One day I was teaching in our church-based Bible School (The International Bible Institute of London). I was talking about vision-building and, since this had been occupying my thoughts, I used our church-planting programme as an example.

'Okay,' I said, 'keep planting churches at the rate we are going, add a pinch of faith and what've we got? Two hundred.'

Wynne Lewis, who was then senior minister of the church, walked past and interrupted.

'Two hundred? It's two thousand, Colin, two thousand!'

'Is that from God?' I asked.

'I don't know, but it sounds good, doesn't it!' he said, and promptly left by plane to fulfil an engagement in Africa.

Several years later, when I took over as senior minister, the figure two thousand began to come back to me. Was this really from God or was it, well, some sort of joke? I needed to know. I sought the Lord. He didn't answer me with a direct 'yes' or 'no' but, over a period of time, he made two aspects of the answer very clear.

The first thing he showed me was that it was possible to expand at that phenomenal rate. This was an achievable goal, not some wild idea that couldn't possibly be realised.

Secondly, he showed me that even if we achieved it he would be unimpressed. I was so shocked. I'd worked out that with an average of fifty people in each satellite church and two thousand churches by the end of the year 2000, we'd have a hundred thousand Christians out there. To sustain that level of church activity I'd thought, just statistically, we would need to be thirty thousand strong in the central church. That was the figure I had felt God had given me and it was confirmed by a word of knowledge from a brother who knew nothing of what I was planning.

A hundred thousand Christians, thirty thousand in a central church and God is unimpressed! I couldn't believe it. I sought him again; I wanted to understand. Then he began to speak to me. I began to see what would happen. Many church leaders in Britain and the rest of Europe are fearful of big visions, considering it boastful and arrogant. But I call it hearing and obeying God. If you intend to partner with God, you'd better get ready for big plans! Anyway, despite their misgivings, people would say, 'This is success. Look at this church growth. How did you do it?' Then there would be the write-ups and the videos – you know how it goes. But God wouldn't have been satisfied at all. And, as I looked at it, I began to see that the real vision was not just to saturate London with little congregations doing their own thing in their own little corner. God showed me something else – what those two thousand churches could do if they stood up as one church, prayed and acted together. This is what the Lord is waiting to see! Think how much more will be achieved when all of God's Church in our cities stand up together and pray in the power and unity of the Spirit. With the right vision and strategy, prayer and planning it can happen.

12   Watchmen Awake!

Failure at Gethsemane

Matthew's Gospel describes how Jesus went to Gethsemane to pray the night before he died (Matthew 26:36–46). He said to Peter and the two sons of Zebedee, 'My soul is overwhelmed with sorrow to the point of death. Stay here and keep watch with me.' Then he moved away a little and fell with his face to the ground, praying, 'My Father, if it is possible, may this cup be taken from me, yet not as I will but as you will.' When he returned to the disciples they were sleeping. 'Could you men not keep watch with me for one hour?' he asked Peter. 'Watch and pray so that you will not fall into temptation. The spirit is willing but the body is weak.'

You would think that this might have woken the disciples up a bit wouldn't you? It didn't. Again Jesus moved away from them to pray. 'My Father,' he said, 'if it is not possible for this cup to be taken away unless I drink it, may your will be done.' When he returned to them they had fallen asleep again because their eyes were heavy.

This time Jesus doesn't wake them but prays again to his Father, accepting the terrible death he is to die the following day, if this is his Father's will. When he comes back to the disciples he finds them still asleep.

'Are you still sleeping and resting?' he says. 'Look, the hour is near, and the Son of Man is betrayed into the hands of sinners.'

I don't believe we can ever fully understand what was going on in Jesus' heart and mind at that time. So often we stress the divinity of Jesus and rightly so, but we must never forget that he was and continues to be also fully man.

Under the shadow of the cross he must have felt the awesome weight of responsibility and the spiritual implications of Calvary. He, who is pure, was about to carry our legacy: all the loathsome impurity of mankind. Jesus, the Son of God, was about to be totally cut off from his Father on our behalf. He is overwhelmed to the point of death before he is even arrested. He knows what is coming and we are told in Luke's gospel that an angel appeared to strengthen him (Luke 22:43–44). The strengthening seemed, however, only to enable him to bear even more anguish and he prayed so earnestly that his sweat dripped to the ground like drops of blood.

We have talked of how the earnest prayer of the righteous avails much with God. How more righteous could a man get than Jesus? How more earnestly could anyone possibly pray? What it must have cost the Father not to allow the cup to pass from him. How much our God loves us!

That night in Gethsemane we see Jesus in need. He is aligning himself, despite his own feelings of dread and revulsion, with the will of his Father in heaven. It is a terrible time, Jesus' darkest hour on earth, and the night before his death. He has asked the disciples, his closest friends, to stand with him in it, to help him, to support him, to pray with him. But those whom he had chosen, loved, nurtured and painstakingly instructed for three and a half years didn't even watch with him for one hour.

That hour of trial is over but I still sense urgency in the Lord's voice as he asks me, all of us, to watch and pray with him now. And it's not always easy. After twenty-five years I still find watching and praying on a daily basis a struggle. It's easy to be enthusiastic in meetings, carried on a tide of prayer, or to pray earnestly when you feel desperate yourself. When my alarm clock goes off early in the morning for my hour of watch, the flesh feels very weak indeed. Then words of Jesus ring in my ears, 'Could you not watch with me for one hour?'

We need to respond to Jesus' voice, to break through this spirit of prayerlessness and be rid of it! Only then can we come into a new level of discipline and urgency in the power of the Holy Spirit. This is a decisive hour of history and there is much that Christ wants to accomplish through us, his bride. Are we going to stand up and watch with him or shall we fail him again, like his disciples did in that night of agony at Gethsemane all those years ago?

A station on the ramparts

'I will stand at my watch and station myself on the ramparts, I will look to see what he will say to me, and what answer I am to give to this complaint' (Habakkuk 2:1).

Habakkuk was a prophet called to minister to God's people at a crucial time in the history of the nation of Judah. The Babylonian empire was growing and threatening to engulf all the neighbouring states of the Middle East, including Judah. Habakkuk seeks God.

He complains that he has called on the Lord and yet the Lord has not responded. He has cried out concerning the violence and destruction coming upon the land; the injustice, the strife and the conflict that he seems.

He tells God how all Israel's laws are paralysed because the wicked pervert justice all the time.

The Lord replies that he is raising up the Babylonian empire against his people to bring judgement on them. Habakkuk's reply is that this is hardly fair because Babylon is even more wicked than God's people. The Lord, however, had no intention of ignoring the sins of Babylon. It is just that judgement begins with the household of God.

Habbakkuk took his station on the ramparts; he was a watchman, alert to what God was doing, questioning the Lord and receiving revelation about the times in which he lived. Like him we need to be taking up our positions, watching what God is doing among the nations and praying according to his revealed will. It is no use praying for peace if God is sending his judgement, or for an end to recession if recession is the Lord's judgement on a materialistic and covetous generation who worship money. In this event perhaps it would be more in keeping to pray for things to get worse, in order to bring nations to their knees.

We need to be able to see what God is doing and not make a god out of our own comfort, putting our needs and considerations first. God's purposes are far higher than that. It's not that the Lord isn't concerned about our needs but the greatest agenda is to see his name honoured, his kingdom come and his will done. This goes right against the grain of what many people expect from a life of prayer.

Great prophets; great prayers

All the great prophets were great prayers. You have to have the heart of an intercessor to bring the word of God to people because it really is not a comfortable thing to do. Isaiah was a watchman and an intercessor. 'For Zion's sake I will not keep silent, for Jerusalem's sake I will not remain quiet, till her righteousness shines out like the dawn, her salvation like a blazing torch' (Isaiah 62:1).

And the Lord speaks through Isaiah concerning the intercessory role of the watchman. 'God says, "I have posted watchmen on your walls, O Jerusalem. They will never be silent day or night. You who call on the LORD, give yourselves no rest, give him no rest until he establishes Jerusalem and makes her the praise of the earth"' (Isaiah 62:6–7).

From the high ramparts of the city wall a watchman can see what is coming, good or bad. The prophets hear from God and are expected to tell the people what they hear. Watchmen are called to proclaim from their vantage point of prophetic revelation. There are two aspects to this proclamation. The first is telling God's people about the wonderful things we see God doing in the heavenly places, so that we can praise him and thank him for his faithfulness to us. The second aspect of proclamation is bringing warning from God concerning the spiritual state of the Church and the nation.

If we believe there is something wrong with what's happening around us, we in the Western nations are all free to be active in expressing our opinions by writing, protesting and petitioning state leaders. If we feel strongly about something, so we should. But who is on the throne of heaven? Should we not be even more concerned with petitioning the one who rules continents?

We have a great responsibility to seek God, interceding for ourselves, our families, our churches and our nation. And we have an equal responsibility to obey God and not keep silent when he speaks to us. We must take our stand and speak the Word of the Lord to our society with authority, clarity and conviction. 'Son of man, I have made you a watchman for the house of Israel, so hear the word I speak and give them warning from me' (Ezekiel 3:17).

Lift up your voices

'Listen! Your watchmen lift up their voices; together they shout for joy. When the LORD returns to Zion, they will see it with their own eyes.' (Isaiah 52:8).

Here the prophet Isaiah speaks of the watchmen leading the way in the praises of God. Watchmen don't have to be gifted singers or musicians. They aren't worship leaders particularly, but when God begins to move they are the first to see it because of their place of watch upon the high walls of the city.

That's what will happen to you if you take up the challenge to be a watchman. It's so much easier to rejoice and praise God when you can see what he is doing. Not only has he sent his Son to redeem us, he is working out his purposes in our real time here on the earth through us. We are in partnership with a great God who is not leaving us to stew in our own failures, our own sins. Whatever our past failings, he is calling us afresh: his desire is that we turn again to him and, in him, find our place of true fulfilment.

The evidence is that the watchmen of today are rejoicing; the prophetic people are hearing from God and praising him. They see the potential of the coming revival; they see it with the eye of faith. They acknowledge it. It's real, it's happening and if we keep seeking God, it's going to come down from the heavenlies to the earth.

Today the Holy Spirit is sweeping across the nations of the world as never before in history. More than one hundred and ten thousand people are added to the Church of Jesus Christ daily. The outpouring is already reaching revival proportions in many different places on practically every continent on earth. And this is only the beginning! We are standing on the edge of the greatest wave of spiritual blessing that has ever been experienced on the earth. The winds are beginning to glow and the flood-tide is about to be released. That is why God is awakening his people to the urgent need of the hour: world-wide prayer and intercession. Only when we pray, will the Lord speak to us. Only when we intercede on behalf of our cities and nations will we see God move in power. He will challenge, inspire and lead us back to himself in real repentance and restoration.

And what of Western Europe? From the outside it may appear that Christianity is on the decline. Empty, outward Church connections are definitely disappearing, but a leaner, fitter Church is emerging where there is a greater correlation between faith and practice.

Church attendance in Great Britain is actually increasing – not uniformly across all denominations – but it is increasing. There is a new unity among leaders from different churches: the streams are coming together; we are beginning to flow in unity of spirit. New streams will joint the current; we are in the process of becoming a mighty river. We must not stand in the way of all this.

Christians today are truly seeking to live what they believe and we are seeing signs of renewal in many places. The Holy Spirit is reversing years of spiritual decline, refreshing and restoring God's people, preparing us for the anointing that is to come when he releases us into new ministries.

One of our ministers was travelling by train on the continent when he noticed a large group of English people. He began to talk to them and discovered that they were all witches on their way to a witchcraft convention. The reason they gave for leaving Britain to practise their witchcraft elsewhere was that the level they were seeking to operate in now no longer works in England. They blamed this new spiritual atmosphere on the prayers of the Christians who have been praying and praising God with marches, prayer walks, nights of prayer, intercession and fasting. The result is an opening in the heavenly realms over Great Britain.

In London many people are flocking to Christ. Christianity is growing at a tremendous rate with one borough said to be on line for a 50 per cent Christian population by the year 2,000. I believe these are the beginnings of a revival that will soon be clearly seen in our city. Many people focus on the threat of God's judgement and say, 'Where is the revival?' If we only view things from an earthly perspective there is a lot to discourage us, but come and stand with me on the ramparts – your view will be quite different. What's more, real prayer and turning to the Lord will be the best possible route to averting judgement and bringing blessing to our nation.

Guard the city

One of the key functions of a watchman was to guard the city. He was the first line of defence because he was high up; he could see what was coming, things still out of sight to those who lived within the city walls. When enemy troops approach the watchman can see them when they are still far off. He is able to warn the inhabitants of the city so that they can get ready to defend themselves. The city cannot be taken by surprise and routed. 'Unless the Lord builds the house, its builders labour in vain. Unless the Lord watches over the city, the watchmen stand guard in vain' (Psalm 127:1).

The Lord is the real watchman. To try to watch in our own strength is fruitless; we are called to watch with him in the Spirit through prayer. Just as watchmen were stationed to protect the city so we, watching with the Lord, are stationed to protect key ministries and events in the body of Christ.

The Lord is raising up men and women who will move not just with words but with mighty demonstration in the power of the Holy Spirit. They need protection and help more than we can ever know. If Jesus, the Lord of glory asked his disciples to watch and pray with him for one hour, how much more do today's spiritual leaders need it?

Whenever men and women take their stand for the Lord they become special targets of the enemy. Agents of the enemy often infiltrate our church services with malevolent aims against the leadership. This especially true of leaders who are particularly effective for God. If you see any Christian in the public eye, or if you see anybody being powerfully used of God in any way at all, pray for them. Cover them. Watch and stand guard over them in prayer. Give them all the spiritual protection you can.

Never forget that our true enemies are spiritual. We are not fighting simply against flesh and blood but against people who have, wittingly or unwittingly, given themselves over to spiritual forces. Just as we can find the Lord moving in unlikely places, touching what at first may have appeared to us the most unlikely of people. Without the insight and discernment of a watchman we can find the enemy opposing us in ways we never anticipated.

The Holy Spirit is raising up a spiritually militant church who will know how to deal with the floodtide of sin. Our weapons are spiritual and prayer is our protective covering as we move forward.

In wartime the numbers of watchmen are doubled and redoubled. There is an intense spiritual war going on right now over the nations of the world. It is essential that watchmen take up their positions both to defend the Church against the onslaught and to go on the offensive against Satan's positions.

Although he is very powerful, we know that Satan and his minions are already defeated. God has equipped us and he's training our hands for battle, to be on the attack and inflict great damage to the enemy. With the high praises of God in our mouths, with the two-edged sword of God's Word in our hands, we go forward to execute God's written judgement on our enemy.

Open the gate

It is the watchman's job to let the gatekeeper know when someone is approaching. They can then find out who it is and, if appropriate, the gates will be opened. It is the watchman who prepared the way for those who want to enter the city.

Jesus uses a similar illustration when he tells the familiar story of the Good Shepherd. Watchmen were used to guard flocks of sheep. The shepherds would go out into the fields, feed their sheep and then come in at evening time and all the flocks would be mingled together in a very large sheep pen. Then the shepherds would leave their sheep in the hands of watchmen who would guard and protect them during the night.

When morning came the shepherds would return. The watchman would open the gate and each shepherd would stand and call his flock. The sheep always knew their own shepherd's voice; they had learned to recognise the sound of the man who fed and cared for them. As soon as they heard him they would follow him out to fresh pasture. It is a principle that still applies in middle-eastern shepherding today.

The watchman opens the gate for him and the sheep listen to his voice. He calls his own sheep by name and leads them out (John 10:3). I believe there is an exciting truth here. The watchman ministry opens the gate for Jesus! Wherever we live, whatever our city, if we fulfil our mandate to watch and pray, the gates will be opened as Jesus approaches. He will come to our cities; he will call his sheep by name and set them free. His sheep will hear his voice and there will be a mass turning to the Lord. This is revival!

God wants you to hear the voice of Jesus as he calls you to take your position seriously and be faithful in prayer. This isn't a call to some sort of elite group; there is no special breed of watchman. This is a call to all of us who know and love the Lord and yearn to see his purposes coming to pass in the earth.

In our own strength we can do nothing; we are only effective as we are empowered by the Holy Spirit. Together we have authority to tread down every work of Satan and we can do all things through Christ who strengthens us. We fight with the Word of the Lord which never returns to him void but accomplishes what he desires and achieves the purpose for which he sent it.

Watch and pray!

In 1989 Billy Graham visited London. In the lead-up to his campaign of evangelism local churches were mixing and local leaders were starting to meet together.

There was a great unity of purpose among us. Billy noticed it.

'Where there is unity at work, God will begin to move,' he said.

Scripture tells us in no uncertain terms how lovely, how pleasing it is, how it delights our hearts and that of our Lord when brothers live together in unity. 'For there the LORD bestows his blessing, even life for ever more' (Psalm 133:3).

Billy came and went but out of that unity a move of God began. Leaders in London particularly said, 'We'll keep meeting together.' There was consultation in different boroughs to discuss how London leaders could do this; everywhere it was prayer, prayer, prayer. We began to meet and pray together four times a year in central venues. Recently we invited all our church members to gather together at Westminster Chapel. About two and a half thousand people came.

This united, corporate praying together has been a feature here in London for several years now. I meet regularly with a group of people called 'London for Jesus' who hold at least one annual celebration each year at the Royal Albert Hall or Wembley Arena. The agenda that everyone wants to follow is one of prayer. People want to come out and pray. In fact, more people will come out to pray than to hear a popular speaker. We are beginning to learn the truth of that psalm first-hand. When those in spiritual authority join together to pray, there is true unity in the Spirit and it is there the Lord bestows his blessing!

Everywhere I go in the world I hear the same call of the Holy Spirit, 'Watch and pray!' And the nations are responding. Ministering in Africa, Asia and South America, I have personally witnessed the new spirit of prayer that is being poured out from the throne of God. The same is becoming true of the European

Church as we are learning to pray with diligency and fervency. As God's day for the nations dawns, the burning question on my heart is will he find us awake and ready or fast asleep and prayerless?

Satan is trying to lay a comfortable blanket over our churches, seeking to induce a spirit of slumber and complacency, because he knows how much danger his kingdom is in when God's people become militant in prayer. We must not allow the enemy to put us to sleep or we shall miss what God is doing, we shall wake up one day to find our lamps without oil.

This is the hour of the watchmen! Watching and praying means praying with your eyes open. Alert and aware of his plans and purposes, we shall actively bring about the will of God in the earth, preparing the way for everything Jesus wants to accomplish. Even if we have failed in the past he wants us to watch and pray now. He is raising us up as a mighty army, equipping us to be faithful in prayer and intercession.

Pray for the harvest, for labourers, for the whole process of bringing in the harvest. We are in very perilous times but they are also exciting times of challenge for the Christian Church. As we pray and intercede, God will pour out his Spirit and we shall find ourselves moving in very strong, very high levels of power, authority, prayer, intercession and evangelism – getting the job done. Despite the enemy's best efforts, this gospel of the kingdom will be preached as an effective witness in all the world!

So, watchmen, hear your summons. Rise up! Stand at your posts! Watch and pray! Amen.